Guiding Rights

2004

Guiding Rights

✦

Trademarks, Copyright and the Internet

Mark V.B. Partridge

iUniverse, Inc.

New York Lincoln Shanghai

Guiding Rights
Trademarks, Copyright and the Internet

All Rights Reserved © 2003 by Mark V.B. Partridge

iUniverse, Inc.

For information address:
iUniverse, Inc.
2021 Pine Lake Road, Suite 100
Lincoln, NE 68512
www.iuniverse.com

ISBN: 0-595-29055-8 (pbk)
ISBN: 0-595-65957-8 (cloth)

Printed in the United States of America

For my wife, Mary

Contents

PREFACE. xi

Part I   *COPYRIGHT*

CHAPTER 1   UNDERSTANDING SUBSTANTIAL
             SIMILARITY AND SCOPE OF PROTECTION . . . 3

CHAPTER 2   INSUFFICIENT EVIDENCE OF
             ORIGINALITY 6

CHAPTER 3   DAMAGES FOR EXTRATERRITORIAL
             COPYRIGHT INFRINGEMENT. 9

CHAPTER 4   CHOICE OF LAW IN INTERNATIONAL
             COPYRIGHT DISPUTES 12

CHAPTER 5   THE KEY DIMENSIONS OF THE FAIR USE
             DEFENSE. 15

CHAPTER 6   COMPARATIVE ADVERTISING AND THE
             FAIR USE DEFENSE. 18

CHAPTER 7   DETERMINING COPYRIGHT DAMAGES 21

CHAPTER 8   COPYRIGHT PREEMPTION ON THE
             INTERNET 25

CHAPTER 9   DERIVATIVE WORKS IN THE DIGITAL
             AGE 28

CHAPTER 10   INFRINGEMENT AS THE KEY TO RIGHTS
             IN DERIVATIVE WORKS 31

Chapter 11   THE LIMITATION PERIOD FOR
COPYRIGHT CLAIMS 34

Chapter 12   THE FIRST SALE DOCTRINE............... 37

Chapter 13   THREATS OF LITIGATION 39

Part II   TRADEMARK

Chapter 14   UNITED STATES TRADEMARK LAW IN
BRIEF 43

Chapter 15   LIKELIHOOD OF CONFUSION:
UNDERSTANDING TRADEMARK LAW'S
KEY PRINCIPLE 46

Chapter 16   TRADE DRESS PROTECTION AND THE
PROBLEM OF DISTINCTIVENESS 56

Chapter 17   USING PATENTS AND COPYRIGHTS TO
CREATE STRONG BRANDS............... 69

Chapter 18   TRADEMARK LICENSING IN A
CORPORATE TRANSACTION.............. 78

Chapter 19   KEY LICENSING CONSIDERATIONS........ 85

Chapter 20   VALIDITY OF REGISTRATION NOT
REVIVED AFTER ABANDONMENT 89

Chapter 21   TRADEMARK PARODY AND THE FIRST
AMENDMENT: HUMOR IN THE EYE OF
THE BEHOLDER 92

Part III   INTERNET

Chapter 22   DOMAIN NAME DISPUTE RESOLUTION:
DEVELOPMENT AND PHILOSOPHY....... 103

Part IV   STRATEGY AND TACTICS

Chapter 23   TO SUE OR NOT TO SUE................. 113

ABOUT THE AUTHOR 123
NOTES 125

PREFACE

"They can't do that. We have a patent on the copyright in that trademark." This quote reflects the general confusion surrounding intellectual property rights, an increasingly regrettable situation as these rights gain importance and prominence in our modern times.

As a law professor, practicing attorney and frequent speaker on these topics, I am often given the chance to attempt an explanation of the legal issues involving intellectual property rights. Typically the audience is limited to a small room of listeners at a convention hotel, a dozen students in a classroom, a handful of readers of a professional journal. With the help of the Internet, some of my past articles have become available to a wider audience, and I have been gratified to learn from time to time that past articles remain helpful to some who stumble upon them on the Internet superhighway. Recently, a business in Denmark contacted me because it saw one of the articles included here on the Internet. This occasional reaction leads me to the hope that the publication of the articles in this collected form may benefit the profession and general public by increasing the overall understanding of the guiding rights that define and protect intellectual property in our Internet Age.

In my effort to understand these legal issues I have been helped and encouraged by many. I would particularly like to recognize the encouragement, inspiration and support I have received from my partners and colleagues at Pattishall, McAuliffe, Newbury, Hilliard and Geraldson. During over twenty-two years with the law firm, I have been privileged to be mentored and taught by some of the finest lawyers and legal experts imaginable and to debate the issues with some of the brightest minds to practice law. Among the chief benefits of my association with that firm are the relationships with clients who confront the cutting edge issues of the day. Their challenging assignments and questions have often provided the foundation to pursue a greater depth of understand of these legal issues. Another benefit is the daily assistance of Nancy Chapman, to whom I owe a constant debt of thanks.

I am also grateful for the inspiration I receive from my students at John Marshall Law School, where I have been honored to teach as an adjunct professor for over fifteen years. It is often stated that the best means of learning is to teach. I have learned much from teaching. I also wish to thank my former students Chuck Wulf and Brian McGraw for their assistance with this project.

Finally, I want to acknowledge my friends and colleagues at the American Intellectual Property Law Association, where I have served as a member, committee chair, meeting planner and member of the Board of Directors. I have profited much from the opportunities and friendships enjoyed as a result of my involvement with that excellent Association.

Chicago, 2003

PART I
COPYRIGHT

1

UNDERSTANDING SUBSTANTIAL SIMILARITY AND SCOPE OF PROTECTION

Reported copyright decisions often reflect a misunderstanding of "substantial similarity" and "scope of protection." The proper application of these key principles can help you shape a copyright infringement case to your best advantage.

SUBSTANTIAL SIMILARITY

The term "substantial similarity" causes confusion in the copyright infringement analysis because the same term has different meanings at two different points in the infringement analysis.

To prove infringement, the plaintiff must show that the defendant copied elements of a work that are original.[1] The *Feist* test for infringement established by the Supreme Court involves two separate inquires. First, did the defendant actually copy the plaintiff's work. Second, were the copied elements protected expression and sufficiently important to be actionable. In other words, did the copying constitute infringement. The term "substantial similarity" is used by the courts for both inquires, but has a different meaning in each instance.

The first prong of the infringement test—actual copying—can be established by showing access to the work and substantial similarity. Here, substantial similarity means that the works are in fact sufficiently similar to support a conclusion that one was actually copied from the other. This involves a relatively low threshold: substantial similarity for the purpose of showing actual copying involves a comparison of the works in their entirety, including protectable and unprotected elements.

The second prong of the infringement test also involves a showing of "substantial similarity" but the meaning is very different. Here, the question is limited to similarities of protected expression. The bar is higher, requiring a showing that the defendant copied a substantial amount of protectable expression.

Problems can arise in litigation when the wrong definition of "substantial similarity" is used. For example, if the court uses the first definition for the second prong of the infringement analysis, the defendant suffers. The court may incorrectly find infringement based on the works as a whole, without determining if the copying involves protectable expression. Similarly, if the court applies the second definition to evaluate the question of actual copying, the failure to consider the works as a whole may disadvantage the plaintiff.

Recognizing the confusion caused by the use of the same term for two different tests, some courts have suggested a distinction between probative or factual similarity on the one hand and substantial or legal similarity on the other.[2] According to this line of cases, the first prong involves probative similarity: whether as a matter of fact, the similarities show actual copying. Under the second prong, the inquiry into substantial similarity is primarily a legal conclusion: whether there are substantial similarities of protected expression sufficient to support a finding of infringement.

Although helpful, the distinction between probative similarity and substantial similarity is not widely stated in reported decisions. Since few courts have a regular docket of copyright infringement matters, litigators should ensure that the court is fully informed about the different definitions of substantial similarity arising in a copyright infringement action, particularly when the difference may have an effect on the client's position.

SCOPE OF PROTECTION

A second area of confusion involves the scope of protection afforded protectable expression in copyright infringement actions. Not all works are entitled to the same level of protection. This issue is particularly important when the works involve a compilation of otherwise unprotectable elements.

The constitutional requirement of originality precludes protection for facts, and the copyright statute precludes protection of "any idea, procedure, process, system, method of operation, concept, principle or discovery."[3] Nevertheless, the "selection, coordination or arrangement" of such unprotectable elements may be entitled to protection if the selection and arrangement has a minimal degree of creativity.

The scope of protection granted to a compilation of unprotectable elements is less than the protection afforded to elements protectable in their own right. It is sometimes said that compilations and factual works are only entitled to "thin" protection, but what does this mean?

According to the Second Circuit, one of the most experienced courts in dealing with copyright issues, a compilation is not infringed if the defendant's work differs in more than a "trivial degree" from the plaintiff's work.[4]

In other courts, the "thin" protection afforded compilations means no relief unless the works are "virtually identical."[5]

In practice, the "trivial difference" test and the "virtually identical" standard have the same result. The plaintiff's burden is higher when seeking protection for compilations of unprotectable elements, and the defendant may escape liability if the works differ by more than a trivial degree. If the plaintiff's work involves elements protectable in their own right, there will be a lower test for infringement. In such cases, the defendant will be liable if the works are found to be substantially similar, as that term is understood in the second prong of the infringement test discussed above.

CONCLUSION

In the abstract world of copyright litigation, the formulation of the tests applied by the court to determine infringement can have a major impact on the outcome of the case. Much may turn on whether the judge or jury is asked to determine if works are substantially similar as a whole or only with respect to protectable elements. Likewise, the results may differ if the fact finder is instructed to determine that the works are virtually identical rather than substantially similar. An understanding of these different tests is important for successful litigation.

2

INSUFFICIENT EVIDENCE
OF ORIGINALITY

A decision of the Tenth Circuit in *TransWestern Publishing Co. LP v. Multimedia Marketing Associates Inc.* demonstrates the importance of providing specific evidence of original contribution when seeking protection of a compilation.[1]

TransWestern published a combined white and yellow pages telephone directory for Ponca City and nearby towns, including advertisements. Account executives solicited the advertisements, prepared ad layout sheets with customer input and created an arrangement of information that was "pleasing to the eye."

Multimedia published a Ponca City community directory, including a number of advertisements that were "very comparable" to those found in the TransWestern directory.

In the lower court, TransWestern obtained a preliminary injunction. At the permanent injunction hearing, however, the lower court granted Multimedia's motion for judgment as a matter of law.

The Court of Appeals began its review with a discussion of the protection available for compilations. Following the Supreme Court's decision in *Feist Publications, Inc. v. Rural Telephone Service Co.*, the court stated that the protection available for a compilation is "thin," since a compilation gains protection through "only minimal creativity in the selection and arrangement of facts."[2] Accordingly, more similarity is required to show infringement. The court noted the comments of commentators and other courts indicating that infringement of a compilation requires "supersubstantial similarity," "virtual identity," or "extensive verbatim copying."

There were many differences between the works as a whole, so that no one would mistake the Multimedia directory for the TransWestern directory. The Court found the directories to be very different in appearance. Although they included similar information, the format, layout and content were different.

6

Given the "thin" protection afforded compilations, the court concluded that it must affirm the district court's finding of no infringement regarding the compilations as a whole.

The court then considered infringement of the specific ads and focused on TransWestern's obligation to present evidence of creative contributions to the copied material. It was here that TransWestern failed to meet its burden of proof. At the permanent injunction hearing, TransWestern presented one witness, an account executive, and seven exhibits, including the registration certificate, the two directories, layout sheets for three advertisements, and a comparison of similar portions of the directories.

TransWestern's account executive testified that he worked with the customer to prepare the advertisements and created the ads shown in the layout sheets. On cross-examination, he claimed his contribution involved "certain logos." When pressed, he acknowledged that the logos were merely words in block print and went on to reveal minimal contributions at best.

> Q. Apart from the names...did you contribute any other artwork to any of the ads?
> A. Artwork meaning pictures, no. Artwork meaning making them pleasing to the eye, yes.
> Q. That would be in the way it was typed, right, the size and style of the type?
> A. Either that, yes, or just saying something to catch the eye.
> Q. But pictures and logos, you wouldn't have anything to do with that, would you?
> A. No, I did not draw pictures.

On redirect, he explained he took the information and artwork from the customer and "arranged and designed it into the ad."

The court was not impressed, dismissing the account executive's testimony as "vague" and insufficient to allow determination of the plaintiff's original contribution to the advertisement. The court rejected the plaintiff's invitation to make its own comparison of the ads to determine infringement, stating:

> To find original and hence protectable contributions by plaintiff to its yellow page ads the court would have to credit the vague and general testimony of the witness that he 'arranged' information provided by his customers and 'designed' the ads—without himself providing any of the artwork—although he did not identify how his contribution was original in any particular ad allegedly copied by defendants. Thus, even if we were to accept plaintiff's

request to compare the allegedly infringing ads for their similar order and placement of information and art work we cannot qualitatively analyze plaintiff's contribution.

The court went on in dicta to consider whether TransWestern's copyright in the compilation as a whole would even afford protection in the advertisements. Treating the directory as a collective work, the court relied on the advertising exclusion in Section 404(a) to conclude that the copyright in the collective work was not applicable to the individual advertisements. This analysis, however, was not necessary to the outcome, given lack of evidence on originality. The court affirmed the lower court's decision by holding that TransWestern "failed to present evidence of its original contributions to the advertisements in question." As a result, the ads were not protectable.

It is, of course, impossible to know from the decision whether the vague testimony of the account executive was the best that could be offered. Perhaps more particularity would have revealed an absence of original contribution. Nevertheless, the decision suggests some important lessons for compilation cases.

For the plaintiff, protection is not likely to be established merely by waving a copyright registration before the court in hope that someone will salute. When dealing with works that contain preexisting or otherwise unprotectable elements, it is a tactical mistake to concentrate solely on the similarity of the works to show infringement, no matter how striking that similarity may be. No infringement exists unless you succeed in proving that the similarities involve protectable expression. In other words, be prepared to show what original contributions you have made to the content, selection or arrangement of material in which you are claiming rights. Similarly, be prepared to show the specific similarities that involve infringement of protectable expression. Do not expect the finder of fact to make the determination on its own simply by examining the works. The court needs your guidance to rule in your favor and will not be pleased if you ask it to do your job.

For the defendant, the lesson is equally clear. Push the plaintiff during discovery to specify its original contribution to the work in which it claims rights, any preexisting elements in which it cannot claim rights and the similarities of protectable expression it believes are infringed. If the plaintiff relies on vague generalities or mere reference to the works at issue, the case may be ripe for summary judgment at the close of discovery or a directed verdict at the close of the plaintiff's case.

3

DAMAGES FOR EXTRATERRITORIAL COPYRIGHT INFRINGEMENT

In today's global market, injury for copyright infringement will often transcend national boundaries. As a result, copyright litigators must understand the territorial limits on copyright protection. Although the U.S. Copyright Laws do not have extraterritorial application, the copyright holder may still recover damages for extraterritorial injury when at least one act of infringement is completed within the United States. The following decisions address the extraterritorial reach of the Copyright Act and help illustrate these black letter principles.

Los Angeles News Service v. Reuters Television International Ltd., decided by the Ninth Circuit Court of Appeals, involved infringement of the copyright in videotapes of the Reginald Denny beating in Los Angeles.[1] When the plaintiffs broadcast the video, the defendants made a copy and transmitted it to subscribers in Europe and Africa. The district court granted summary judgement dismissing the claims for damages based on the extraterritorial use of the video, finding that "any damages arising extraterritorially are the result of extraterritorial infringement."

On appeal, the court recognized that the established rule (that the Copyright Act does not apply extraterritorially) was limited by a key exception (that the Act applies if there is one complete domestic act of infringement). The question becomes this: May the copyright holder recover damages for international distribution when a predicate act of infringement occurred in the United States? The court considered this to be a question of first impression in the Ninth Circuit, and relied on Second Circuit precedent for guidance.

In the classic case of *Sheldon v. Metro-Goldwyn Pictures Corp.*, Judge Learned Hand, writing for the Second Circuit, held that a plaintiff could recover profits

9

from foreign film exhibition if the infringing copy had been made in the United States.[2] Hand's theory was one of constructive trust. Once the infringing copy was made in the United States, Hand felt the plaintiff possessed an equitable interest in the copy and was entitled to all profits made from it, whether earned in the United States or abroad.

In the *L.A. News* case, the predicate act of infringement in the United States occurred when the defendant made a copy of the video in the United States, enabling exploitation abroad via satellite transmission. When the acts of infringement occur entirely abroad, the extraterritorial limit applies and results in no relief.[3] But because the *L.A. News* infringement occurred in the United States, the plaintiff was entitled to recover all consequential damages, whether arising within or outside the United States.

Within days of the *L.A. News* decision, the Southern District of New York addressed another angle of the extraterritorial enforcement question. The plaintiff in *Quantitative Financial Software, Ltd. v. Infinity Financial Technology, Inc.*, an Israeli corporation, relied on the Berne Convention to assert copyrights in software against a New York corporation for acts of infringement occurring outside the United States.[4]

The court noted that jurisdiction over extraterritorial acts required some act within the United States that infringed the Copyright Act.

In response, the plaintiff relied on three domestic acts: (1) the infringement involved a contract entered in the United States; (2) only defendant's U.S. personnel had the ability to create the infringement; and (3) the infringing software was used by foreign companies to execute transactions in the United States.

None of these facts satisfied the plaintiff's obligation to show a predicate act of infringement within the United States. As a result, the court dismissed the action for lack of subject matter jurisdiction.

The plaintiff apparently also argued that the Berne Convention Implementation Act should confer subject matter jurisdiction over actions for copyright infringement outside the United States. The Court rejected this position, noting that the Implementation Act specifically provides that actions may only be brought under the Copyright Act, or other applicable domestic laws, and not directly under the Berne Convention itself. Thus, U.S. implementation of the Berne Convention does not eliminate the requirement under U.S. law for a predicate act of infringement inside the United States.

Several lessons can be learned from these cases. If an act of infringement has occurred in the United States, do not limit your claim for damages to domestic sales. Foreign sales that directly resulted from the domestic infringement may be included in the damage calculation. Plan your pleadings, discovery and proofs accordingly. The failure to identify a complete act of infringement within the U.S. can be grounds for dismissal.

4

CHOICE OF LAW IN INTERNATIONAL COPYRIGHT DISPUTES

In our global, Internet age, we can expect to face more choice of law issues in copyright litigation. A decision by the United States Court of Appeals for the Second Circuit involving the rights of Russian journalists provides a useful framework for analysis.

Imagine the following scenario: works created in a foreign country by foreign nationals are reproduced and distributed in the United States. The foreign nationals seek relief in a U.S. court. What law applies and how should the case be handled?

This question arose in *Itar-Tass Russian News Agency v. Russian Kurier, Inc.*[1] The plaintiffs included major Russian language newspapers and magazines in Russia, a Russian wire service located in Moscow and a professional writers union located in Russia. The defendant, *Russian Kurier*, created a weekly Russian language newspaper for distribution in New York City using text and pictures cut from the plaintiffs' publications. Thus, there was no dispute as to the actual copying of the plaintiffs' works. The issue turned on whether the plaintiffs had standing, a question that involved choice of law principles and the substantive meaning of Russian copyright law.

CHOICE OF LAW

Choice of law issues have largely been ignored in past copyright decisions, with many courts apparently assuming without analysis that U.S. law applies to determine ownership and infringement for foreign nationals. This is understandable, since the Berne Convention provides that the national of a member state is enti-

12

tled to national treatment in each other member state, and some commentators have concluded that the applicable law is the copyright law of the country where the infringement occurred.

The Court in *Itar-Tass* notes, however, that international copyright cases present two distinct issues: ownership and infringement. National treatment under the Berne Convention merely assures that the national law of infringement will be applied uniformly to foreign and domestic authors; it provides no guidance on the question of ownership. Indeed, the Berne Convention Implementation Act specifically provides that the rights eligible for protection "shall not be expanded or reduced" by virtue of the Berne Convention.[2] Therefore, the Court concludes that traditional choice of law rules determine ownership of rights.

OWNERSHIP OF RIGHTS

Under U.S. choice of law principles, the applicable law for determining interests in property is the law of the state with the most significant relationship to the property and the parties. Since the works were created by Russian nationals and first published in Russia, ownership should be determined by Russian law. The Berne Convention provides nothing to the contrary. The question of ownership also involves the scope and nature of the interest owned. This, too, is determined by Russian law.

Determination of a foreign country's law is an issue of law to be decided by the reviewing court. Relying on the testimony of Russian legal experts, the court found that the Russian version of the work-for-hire doctrine excludes newspapers. Thus, under Russian law the newspaper plaintiffs were not the owners of exclusive rights in the articles at issue. The individual authors retained those rights. The only rights held by the newspapers were compilation rights in the selection, arrangement and presentation of the articles in the newspaper. In contrast, the news agency plaintiff was not excluded from the Russian work-for-hire provision and therefore owned the exclusive rights in the articles written by its employees.

INFRINGEMENT

The applicable law for determining infringement is the location of the harm, the doctrine generally applied to torts. Here, the tort occurred in the United States, so U.S. law applies. It is clear that the defendants violated the exclusive rights of the copyright owners to reproduce and distribute the copyrighted works. The key question then becomes determination of the ownership interests of the various plaintiffs.

RELIEF

Based on the application of the conflicts of law principles, the court reaches an outcome different from that which would have been obtained under U.S. law. Based on the U.S. work for hire doctrine, both the newspaper and the news agency would have owned the rights in the articles created by their employees. However, because of the specific exclusion in the Russian work-for-hire statute, the newspapers did not own the exclusive rights in the articles created by its employees. For this reason, the court affirms the lower court's judgment in favor of the news agency, reverses the judgment in favor of the newspapers and remands for judgment on the right of the union to collect on behalf of its member authors and on the right of the newspapers to recover for infringement of their limited compilation rights.

International copyright problems will become increasingly common for U.S. attorneys as the world becomes a single global marketplace connected by the Internet. We are increasingly likely to face infringements that cross borders and require an analysis like that employed in the *Itar-Tass* case. Plaintiffs should be sure to name as co-plaintiffs the owners of the rights under the applicable national law. Much of the difficulties in the *Itar-Tass* case could have been avoided if the individual authors had been included as plaintiffs or if the newspapers had obtained an assignment of rights. Do not assume that the publisher of the work automatically has ownership and standing to sue. Under U.S. law, only the legal or beneficial owner of an exclusive right in the work has standing to sue. Defendants should also consider the effect of foreign law on the rights at issue as part of their defense strategy.

5

THE KEY DIMENSIONS OF THE FAIR USE DEFENSE

A principal defense in copyright litigation is the fair use exception to copyright found in Section 107 of the Copyright Statute[1]. When evaluating the statutory factors, the key dimensions or aspects of the factual inquiry appear to be transformation, commercial use and market value.

The fair use exception permits reproduction of copyrighted material "for purposes such as criticism, comment, news reporting, teaching (including multiple copies for classroom use), scholarship, or research."[2] This list of purposes is not exhaustive, but merely illustrative of the types of uses that may be deemed fair use.

The fair use doctrine involves a mixed question of law and fact based on a set of statutory factors. These factors stated in Section 107 are:

1.   the purpose and character of the use, including whether such use is of a commercial nature or is for nonprofit educational purposes;

2.   the nature of the copyrighted work;

3.   the amount and substantiality of the portion used in relation to the copyrighted work as a whole; and

4.   the effect of the use upon the potential market for or value of the copyrighted work.

None of these factors is deemed determinative and must be balanced together in making the analysis. Generally, the most critical evidence addresses three key dimensions or aspects of the fair use inquiry: transformation, commercial use and market value.

The Fourth Circuit in *Sundeman v. The Seajay Society, Inc.*[3] applied the fair use defense to the unauthorized reproduction of unpublished works of Marjorie

Kinnan Rawlings Baskin ("Rawlings"), the author of *The Yearling* and other noted books. The Seajay Society, an organization dedicated to enhancing awareness of South Carolina culture, obtained some of Rawling's unpublished works, including Rawling's first novel, *Blood of My Blood*. Dr. Anne Blythe received a copy of the unpublished novel from Seajay, presented an analysis of *Blood of My Blood* at a Society symposium, quoting about four to six percent to the text, and submitted her paper for publication.

The plaintiffs sought damages and injunctive relief for (1) the copy of *Blood of My Blood* given by Seajay to Blythe; (2) a partial copy given by Seajay to the University of Florida; (3) Blythe's presentation which quoted from the work; (4) Blythe's attempt to publish her presentation; and (5) further dissemination of the unpublished novel. Seajay conceded that the copies it made of *Blood of My Blood* constituted copyright infringement unless they were protected by the fair use exception.

Moving beyond an obvious discussion of the four statutory factors, the case reveals three key dimensions that can be used to shape any fair use analysis. Most fair use questions can be resolved by focusing your litigation strategy on these factual issues.

(1) *Transformation*. The first dimension involves the character of the use: Whether the work is transformative or merely supersedes the original. A work is transformative if it adds something new to the original. Although such transformation is not absolutely necessary for a finding of fair use, it does further the purpose of the Copyright Laws and weighs in favor of a finding of fair use.

(2) *Commercial Use*. The second key dimension is the purpose of the use: Whether the defendant intended to profit from the use without proper payment. Again, this factor is not conclusive. Although most of the statutory examples of fair use typically involve some profit motive, the lack of commercial purpose favors a finding of fair use.

(3) *Market Value*. The third key dimension is the effect on the value of the original: Whether the defendant's work will impair the market value of the original work. Any use that supplants the market for the original is unlikely to be considered a fair use.

The facts presented on these dimensions in the *Seajay* case supported a finding of fair use. The Blythe presentation was transformative in that it involved a scholarly appraisal of the work. Although Blythe may have hoped to get royalties for her presentation, her efforts were never published and merely served to benefit the development of the arts. Finally, the presentation would not interfere with sales of the original or inhibit demand for derivative works.

A California case provides another illustrative example. In *Michaels v. Internet Entertainment Group, Inc.*, the defendant argued that it should be permitted by the doctrine of fair use to show excerpts of a sexually explicit video featuring the rock star Bret Michaels and television star Pamela Anderson Lee on its Internet site.[4] The Court concluded that the display of short segments of the video would not be fair use. The result is easily reached based on the facts relating to each of three dimensions discussed above.

The excerpts of the Michaels/Lee video did not involve any transformation of the original work. The defendant's proposed use would be commercial, since it built its subscriber base by offering short video clips for adult entertainment. Finally, the segments of the video were likely to propagate quickly online and saturate the potential market for the copyrighted work.

The Second Circuit provides another example in *Leibovitz v. Paramount Pictures Corporation.*[5] Well-known photographer Annie Liebovitz claimed that an advertisement for the movie *Naked Gun 33 1/3: The Final Insult* infringed her photograph of Demi Moore on the August 1991 cover of *Vanity Fair*. Paramount's photograph featured the face of actor Leslie Neilsen superimposed on the naked body of a pregnant woman posed to look like Moore in the Leibovitz photograph. Following the Supreme Court's decision in *Campbell v. Acuff-Rose Music, Inc.*,[6] the court concluded that the Paramount advertisement was fair use.

The evidence on the dimensions noted above supported a finding of fair use, but was not as definitive as the evidence in *Seajay* or *Michaels*. The Paramount advertisement was transformative because the parody was a new work which commented on the original, and was not merely a copy of the original. Further, Leibovitz conceded that the defendant's work would not interfere with the potential market for her photograph or for derivative works based on it. Finally, the court discounted the commercial nature of the use. After *Campbell*, it can no longer be said that every commercial use of copyrighted material is presumptively unfair. The commercial nature of the use is merely a factor for consideration. The fact that the Paramount advertisement promoted a commercial product weighed against a finding a fair use, but the weight of the evidence on transformation and market value markedly favored the defendant. The Court gave little weight to the evidence relating to the nature of the plaintiff's use or the amount of the taking, both of which seemed to favor Leibovitz.

The key dimensions used to evaluate the fair use factors appear to be transformation, commercial use and market value. By focusing arguments and evidence on these key dimensions, litigants will increase their chances of success when addressing the fair use defense.

6

COMPARATIVE
ADVERTISING AND THE
FAIR USE DEFENSE

Does use of another's copyrighted material in comparative advertising constitute copyright infringement or fair use? In contrast to trademark law, where truthful reference in advertising to another's mark is a common form of fair use under U.S. law, the use of another's copyrighted material in comparative advertising has rarely been addressed by the courts. The Ninth Circuit issued its first decision on the matter in *Sony Computer Entertainment America, Inc. v. Bleem, LLC[1]*. The case provides useful guidelines for persons engaging in comparative advertising.

Bleem markets a software emulator that allows gamers to run Sony PlayStation video games on a personal computer without using a PlayStation console. Gamers benefit because the Bleem software is cheaper than a Sony PlayStation console and a high resolution computer monitor produces better graphics than the typical television monitor used with a console.

To market its emulator, Bleem ran advertising in various media that included comparative screen shots of the Sony PlayStation games showing what the game looked like when played with a Sony console on a television screen versus the appearance of the game on a computer screen using Bleem's emulator.

Sony sued Bleem on various theories and the district court granted a preliminary injunction. On appeal, the only issue was whether Bleem's unauthorized use of the Sony PlayStation game screen shots was a violation of Sony's copyright. Bleem admitted that it copied Sony's copyrighted work, but claimed that its actions were protected as fair use under 17 U.S.C. §107.

The relevant statutory provisions are well known. The fair use exception permits reproduction of copyrighted material "for purposes such as criticism, comment, news reporting, teaching (including multiple copies for classroom use), scholarship, or research."[2] This list of purposes is merely illustrative of the types

18

of uses that may be deemed fair use. The statute sets forth four well-known factors for determining fair use.

On the first factor, although Bleem's activity was commercial, the court noted that any rule presuming unfairness had been eliminated by the Supreme Court in *Campbell v. Accuff-Rose Music, Inc.*[3] Although some courts applied that rule in the past, in holding that a parody of the Roy Orbison song "Pretty Woman" was fair use, the Supreme Court in *Campbell* held that commercial use could not be deemed presumptively unfair. Instead, commercial use is merely a factor to consider in the fair use analysis.

In the *Sony* case, after acknowledging the social utility of comparative, commercial advertising, the court held that the first fair use factor favored the Bleem:

> Although Bleem is most certainly copying Sony's copyrighted material for the commercial purpose of increasing its own sales, such comparative advertising redounds greatly to the purchasing public's benefit with very little corresponding loss to the integrity of Sony's copyrighted material.

The court indicated that the second factor was not much help. Although the video game was creative in nature, the screen shot "was merely an inanimate sliver of the game." Although that distinction explains little, the court dismissed this factor quickly and concluded that it "neither supports nor hurts" the fair use claim.

In the evaluation of the third factor, we learn that a screen shot is "$1/30^{th}$ of a second's worth of a video game" and is "of little substance to the overall copyrighted work." According to the court, in any fair use analysis involving video game screen shots, "the third factor will almost always weigh against the video game manufacturer since a screen shot is such an insignificant portion of the complex copyrighted work as a whole."

The important fourth factor receives the most weight in the analysis. First, the court distinguishes between the market for emulators, which Sony cannot protect, and the market for screen shots, which might be protected. Only the screen shot market is relevant, but there is no market for the screen shots per se. Harm caused by the criticism inherent to comparative advertising is not cognizable. Further, Bleem's use of screen shots in its advertising would have "no noticeable effect on Sony's ability to do with its screen shots what it chooses."

Having found that the four fair use factors favored Bleem, the court then considered whether it should overrule the district court's grant of a preliminary injunction as an abuse of discretion. The Court found the lower court decision to be inadequate. "Upon the record before us, we cannot tell whether the district court engaged in the § 107 analysis and thus we have no evidence of its discretion. In the absence of such an analysis, it does appear that the district court abused its discretion…" As a result, the court vacated the preliminary injunction and remanded.

The *Sony* decision illustrates several useful principles. First, the fair use defense is available even when the defendant's use is commercial and competitive in nature. Second, comparative advertising is a form of criticism and comment, two of the permitted purposes specifically mentioned in the fair use statute. Finally, a prevailing party on a preliminary injunction motion should encourage the court to support its decision with detailed findings of fact and conclusions of law. Although a district court's preliminary injunction decision is entitled to considerable deference, a cursory ruling risks rejection as an abuse of discretion. If the court fails to take the laboring oar, the careful advocate should volunteer to draft a proposed order including adequate findings of fact and conclusions of law.

7

DETERMINING COPYRIGHT DAMAGES

So, the judge found in your favor on liability. Your principal competitor's database program contains elements that infringe your copyrights. How will you fare in the recovery phase? If you failed to register the work before the infringement, perhaps not as well as you hope.

17 U.S.C. §412 provides that "no award of statutory damages or of attorney's fees" shall be made for "any infringement of copyright...commenced before the effective date of the its registration." This provision applies to additional or continuing infringements commencing after registration. "A plaintiff may not recover an award of statutory damages and attorney's fees for infringements that commenced after registration if the same defendant commenced an infringement of the same work prior to registration."[1] There is a three month grace period after publication for timely registration. Because the high cost of litigation can sometimes derail future enforcement efforts, proactive counsel and clients should encourage registration soon after the work is released and should not wait until infringement problems arise.

Without the ability to recover statutory damages and attorney's fees, the prevailing copyright plaintiff is limited to recovering actual damages and profits under 17 U.S.C. §504(b), which permits the copyright owner to recover: "The actual damages suffered by him or her as a result of the infringement, and any profits of the infringer that are attributable to the infringement and are not taken into account in computing actual damages."

ACTUAL DAMAGES

Actual damages equal the profits the plaintiff might have accrued but for the defendant's infringement. The determination of the plaintiff's actual damages is fact-specific, as explained in *Fitzgerald Publishing Co, Inc. v. Baylor Publishing Co, Inc.*:[2]

> The primary measure for the recovery of actual damages under [Section 504(b)] is the extent to which the market value of the copyrighted work at the time of the infringement has been harmed or destroyed by the infringement...The best method available for measuring this diminution in market value is the profit lost by the plaintiff due to the infringements...Further, the profit lost by the plaintiff is not equivalent to the profit gained by the infringers, since the opposing parties will have different selling techniques and business organizations.

There must be a causal relation between the infringement and the diminution of plaintiff's product. Often, the sales of the defendant's product or the lost sales of the plaintiff may be attributable to factors other than the infringement. If, for example, the defendant sells the infringing product at a substantially lower price than the plaintiff sells the copyrighted product, that causal relation may not exist. The judge in *Fedtro, Inc. v. Kravex Manufacturing Corp.*, denied proximate causation on that basis:[3]

> The evidence does not warrant any inference that defendant's copyright infringement was the proximate cause of plaintiff's losses of sales to defendant and others. Plaintiff's price of eighty-nine cents was in the significant trade paths substantially in excess of [defendant's] selling list price of sixty cents and actual sale price of an average of about fifty-five cents. With that differential in price, which the evidence warrants concluding was the dominant difference between the two articles in their trade successes, there is no reason to doubt that defendant's article would have commanded a substantial share of the market whether presented on a display card or in a sack under a header. It is speculation to seek to locate some measurable quantum of sales diversion that can fairly be traced to the use of [the copyrighted materials] rather than to other marketability factors.

Other market factors may have a similar effect: changing technology; third party competition; non-infringing aspects of the infringing product. The plaintiff has the burden of showing the causal connection between the infringement and some loss of anticipated revenue and may not rely on mere speculation. The plaintiff also has the burden of proving the profits it would have made on sales lost as a result of the infringement.

DEFENDANT'S PROFITS

Under 17 U.S.C. §504(b), to establish the infringer's profits, the copyright owner is required to present proof only of the infringer's gross revenue, and the infringer is required to prove his or her deductible expenses and the elements of profit attributable to factors other than the copyrighted work.

In *Design v. K-Mart Apparel Corp.*, the court discussed the application of this provision.[4] The plaintiff must present proof of the defendant's gross revenue. This can be met by showing the number of infringing items sold and the defendant's listed price for those items. The defendant must then prove deductible expenses, and failure to prove deductions could result in an award of gross sales revenue. The available deductions include:

-Difference between actual and list price of goods sold.

-Cost of goods sold.

-Overhead expense. The defendant has the "burden of proving that each item of general expense contributed to the production of the infringing items, and of further offering a fair and acceptable formula for allocating a given portion of overhead to the particular infringing items in issue."[5]

-Income tax paid on profits. This is not deductible where infringement was conscious and deliberate."[6]

Because some of the expenses carried on the defendant's books may not be attributable to the production of the infringing product, profits may be awarded even when the defendant's books or tax returns show a loss.

APPORTIONMENT

In calculating the defendant's profits, there should be a deduction for elements of profits attributable to factors other than the copyrighted work. This can be difficult when non-infringing elements are combined with infringing elements to create a single work: for example, a 400 page novel with 10 infringing pages; infringing lyrics combined with a non-infringing melody; a video with incidental display of infringing photographs.

The seminal case on apportionment is *Sheldon v. Metro-Goldwyn Pictures Corp.*,[7] where the Supreme Court upheld an award of one fifth of the defendant's profits from an infringing motion picture. Holding that apportionment principles of patent law applied fully to copyright cases, the Court stated:

> In so far as the profits from the infringing sales were attributable to the patented improvements they belonged to the plaintiff, and in so far as they were due to other parts or features they belonged to the defendants. But as the drills were sold in completed and operative form, the profits resulting from the several parts were necessarily commingled. It was essential, therefore, that they be separated or apportioned between what was covered by the patent and what as not covered by it...In such case, if plaintiff's patent only created a part of the profits, he is only entitled to recover that part of the net gains.

The Court emphasized that apportionment does not have to be mathematically exact. Only a reasonable approximation is required, to be attained "through the testimony of experts and persons informed by observation and experience."

DOUBLE COUNTING

Finally, remember that the award of the defendant's profits should not include profits taken into account when computing actual damages. As explained by the Seventh Circuit in *Taylor v. Meirick*,[8] if the profits the owner would have made but for the infringement are equal to the profits the infringer made by selling the copyrighted item, and the owner proves up his lost profits, the "not taken into account" clause...bars the owner from receiving an additional award of damages based on the infringer's profits. In other words, double counting is not allowed.

The damages phase of a copyright case can be difficult and time consuming, requiring the testimony of accounting and marketing experts. The difficulties and expense inherent in the effort are strong incentives for early registration so that statutory damages and attorney's fees may be sought as a relatively easy alternative.

8

COPYRIGHT PREEMPTION ON THE INTERNET

The problem of preemption has been the subject of increased discussion as litigators reconsider traditional legal theories to confront new problems in the Internet age.[1] Two useful guides for evaluating the application of preemption to new technology are *Ticketmaster Corp. v. Tickets.com, Inc.*[2] and *eBay, Inc. v. Bidder's Edge, Inc.*[3], both district court decisions from California.

The statutory authority for copyright preemption is found in Section 301 of the Copyright Act, which states, in relevant part:[4]

> [A]ll legal or equitable rights that are the equivalent to any of the exclusive rights within the general scope of copyright...in works of authorship that are fixed in a tangible medium of expression and come with the subject matter of copyright...are governed exclusively by this title...[N]o person is entitled to any such right or equivalent right in any such work under the common law or statutes of any State.

Ticketmaster operates an Internet web site that allows customers to purchase tickets to concerts, ball games and other events. Tickets.com operates a web site that provides information on where tickets can be purchased. Its web site displays a short factual description for the event, including time, date, place and price. One of the issues in the *Ticketmaster* case arose from the defendant's use of computer technology to gather factual information about events from the Ticketmaster site. Ticketmaster alleged, inter alia, that the defendant's conduct was an unlawful trespass under California state law.

To prevail on a trespass claim based on accessing a computer system, a plaintiff must establish (1) the defendant intentionally and without authorization interfered with a possessory interest in the computer system; and (2) the defendant's unauthorized use proximately resulted in damage to plaintiff.[5]

On the defendant's motion to dismiss, the court in *Ticketmaster* considered the scope of preemption, stating that a surviving state claim must have an "extra element" which changes the nature of the claim. Also, if copying is permitted by the Copyright Act, a contrary state law could not be enforced. In other words, a state law that prevents the taking of facts from a copyrighted work could not be enforced unless there was something extra beyond mere copying involved.

The court held that the trespass claim was preempted, stating:

> The essence of [the] claim is the invasion and taking of factual information compiled by Ticketmaster. To the extent that state law would allow protection of factual data (not clear at all), this cannot be squared with the Copyright Act...In addition, it is hard to see how entering a publicly available web site could be called a trespass, since all are invited to enter.

A different result was reached in the *eBay* case, decided two months later. EBay operates an Internet auction site. Bidder's Edge operates a site that consolidates auction information from various sites including eBay and others. It gathers its auction information using a software robot, also known as a spider, robot or web crawler, to search, copy and retrieve information from the web sites of others. Bidder's Edge initially approached eBay to negotiate a license for access to the eBay site, but proceeded without a license when the parties failed to agree on terms. EBay moved for preliminary injunction, claiming that the invasion of its site by Bidder's Edge was an unlawful trespass on chattels under California law.

The court found a sufficient likelihood that eBay would prevail on the trespass claim and granted a preliminary injunction. The court noted that trespass to chattels was recently applied in California to prevent the unauthorized use of long distance telephone lines.[6] Therefore, it appears that electronic signals over the Internet are sufficiently tangible to support a trespass claim.

The trespass involved the use of the automated program to enter eBay's databases, not the unauthorized use of eBay's information. Bidder's Edge had continued the intrusion even when asked by eBay to stop. The fact that the site was publicly accessible did not justify the intrusion. The eBay servers were private property, and eBay explicitly notified automated visitors that their access was not permitted. Thus, Bidder's Edge exceeded the scope of consent granted to persons using the eBay site. The damage to eBay arose from the loss of available bandwidth and server capacity. Although the intrusion may be negligible, if permitted, it could encourage intrusions by others resulting in a substantial impairment.

The court concluded that the trespass claim was not preempted because the rights involved were not the same as those addressed by a copyright claim:

Here, eBay asserts a right not to have [Bidder's Edge] use its computer systems without authorization. The right to exclude others from using physical personal property is not equivalent to any rights protected by copyright and therefore constitutes an extra element that makes trespass qualitatively different from a copyright infringement claim.

The claim is distinguishable from the claim in the *Ticketmaster* decision where the court focused on the unauthorized use of information, rather than on the intrusion into a computer system. While the former appears to involve rights equivalent to copyright, the later does not.

A second, unpublished order on a motion for preliminary judgment was issued in the *Ticketmaster* case. Citing the *eBay* decision with approval, the *Ticketmaster* court concluded that the trespass theory might be applicable to use of spiders and robots to gather online facts from web sites, but denied preliminary relief based on the facts of the case before him:

> The comparative use by [defendant] appears very small and there is no showing that the use interferes to any extent with the regular business of [plaintiff]. If it did, an injunction might well issue…Nor here is the specter of dozens or more parasites joining the fray, the cumulative total of which could affect the operation of TM's business.

These decisions provide a useful point of comparison for drafting trespass claims involving electronic intrusion into computer systems.

9

DERIVATIVE WORKS IN THE DIGITAL AGE

In the new millennium, we are destined to face an increasing number of copyright disputes as agreements created for twentieth century technology confront the digital age.

A case in point is the Ninth Circuit decision in *Mendler v. Winterland Production, Ltd.*[1] As noted by Judge Alex Kozinski, writing for the majority, the case addresses the following riddle: "When is a photograph no longer a photograph?"

Jeffrey Mendler, a professional photographer, took photographs of the America's Cup yacht race in San Diego. In 1991, he licensed a number of images to Winterland, a manufacturer of screen-printed apparel for use as "guides, models, and examples, for illustrations to be used on screenprinted T-shirts or other sportswear." Winterland soon began marketing T-shirts under this agreement featuring drawings based on Mendler's photograph. Winterland sent Mendler samples, and there was no further communication between them for several years.

In 1995, Mendler encountered a new line of America's Cup T-shirts from Winterland featuring the same scene as the early shirts. Instead of drawings, however, the new shirts displayed a digitally altered version of Mendler's original photograph.

Mendler objected to the images on the new shirts. When negotiations failed, he filed suit for copyright infringement and related claims.

The district court, deciding the case without a jury, dismissed Mendler's claim after trial and held that Winterland's use of the slides was within the scope of the license agreement. On appeal, the Ninth Circuit reversed and remanded that decision.

Contract interpretation is a question of law reviewed de novo, particularly where the trial court does not rely on extrinsic evidence to interpret an ambiguous contract. In this case, both parties agreed that the contract did not authorize Winterland to use photographic reproductions of Mendler's work. Thus, to affirm the district court, the court of appeals had to find that the new image on the T-shirt was not a photograph. This is where the two tribunals tack opposite courses.

To create the new images on the T-shirts, Winterland scanned Mendler's photograph into its computer system creating a digital reproduction. Then, using Adobe Photoshop software, Winterland flipped the image, reconstructed the end of a cropped off sail, replaced the original sky with clouds, changed colors and compressed the entire tonal range of the image through a process called posterization. Winterland claimed this digital manipulation was no longer the photograph itself but an image based on the photograph. The terms of the license that permitted use of the photographs as "guides, models, and examples, for illustrations..." Thus the riddle: was the image a photograph or an illustration based on a photograph?

To resolve this question, the court sought supplemental briefing from the parties on the history of photography and the nature of the computer technology used to create the new image. The resulting decision is filled with facts about photographic manipulation.

The majority recognizes that Winterland would not have violated the license if it had hired a skilled artist to create the same image it ultimately created. The majority also recognizes that Winterland was free to make an illustration by scanning Mendler's photograph and using computer software to digitally alter the photograph to create an illustration. However, the majority concludes that digital manipulation imposed an added burden:

> In choosing this method rather than reconstructing the image from scratch, however, Winterland necessarily took on a burden of altering the image sufficiently so it would no longer exhibit those qualities that cause us to recognize it as a photograph. This must be so, for if the use of a photographic process to reach a recognizably photographic result is authorized, the parties' avowed understanding that photographic reproductions are not 'illustrations' becomes meaningless.

Comparing Mendler's photograph with Winterland's altered image, the court finds that essential aspects of the original photograph remained visible and unaltered. As a result, Winterland's use of the photo exceeded the scope of the license and infringed Mendler's copyright.

The dissent rejects the majority's use of photography information not contained in the record. Having studied the record, the dissent is not convinced that the district court erred in finding the new image to be within the scope of the license because the contract allowed Winterland to "use whatever illustration process it finds most appropriate." It does not exclude computer-scanned images as "guides, models, and examples" for computer created artwork, even though scanning technology was available at the time.

I share the dissent's surprise at the majority's reliance on information outside the record to shape its interpretation of the contract. There is no way of knowing whether this information affected the parties' intent when entering into the contract. One also notes the degree to which the majority rests its conclusion on the concession of counsel that the contract did not permit Winterland to use photographic reproductions of Mendler's photo. As noted by the dissent, the contract is not that specific. And that, of course, is why the dispute arose in the first place.

10

INFRINGEMENT AS THE KEY TO RIGHTS IN DERIVATIVE WORKS

Conflicts involving two derivative works sometimes involve disputes that seem impossible to adjudicate. Does the second derivative work copy the first derivative work or the original? The Seventh Circuit decision *Pickett v. Prince* is a useful guide for sorting through the difficulties inherent in derivative work disputes.[1]

The case involves the copyright in a derivative work based on the unpronounceable symbol used by the singer now once again known as Prince. The singer's name at birth was Prince Rogers Nelson. For many years he performed under the name Prince. In 1992, he began referring to himself by an unpronounceable symbol resembling the Egyptian hieroglyph "ankh". The symbol served as his trademark and as a copyrighted work of visual art that Prince licensed to others. The copyright in the symbol was registered in 1997, but the copyright dates back to the symbol's creation in 1992.

In 1993, Ferdinand Pickett made a guitar in the shape of the symbol, which he apparently showed to the singer. Afterwards, Prince began using a similar guitar in public performances, and Pickett filed suit.

The district court granted Prince's motion for summary judgment on the ground that Pickett had no right to make a derivative work based on the symbol without Prince's consent. On appeal, Pickett claimed "the right to copyright a work derivative from another person's copyright without that person's permission and then to sue that person for infringement by the person's own derivative work."

The logic of Pickett's argument is based on statute. Section 101 of the Copyright Act defines a derivative work as: "A work based on one or more preexisting works [including] any form in which a work may be recast, transformed, or adapted."[2]

Section 103(b) provides that the copyright in a derivative work "extends only to the material contributed by the author of such work, as distinguished from the preexisting material employed in the work, and does not imply any exclusive right in the preexisting material. The copyright in such work is independent of…any copyright protection in the preexisting material"[3]

Based on these principles, Picket asserts that he has recast the symbol in a new form and that he is entitled to protect the incremental originality in that new creation. The court acknowledges the possibility that Pickett's efforts may involve some incremental originality, stating: "Maybe, though, the juxtaposition of the symbol and the guitar is enough to confer on the ensemble sufficient originality as a work of visual art to entitle the designer to copyright it."

That being true, Pickett asserts that he owns a valid copyright in that incremental originality that he contributed to the preexisting work. Further, he asserts that Prince infringed his copyright by creating a guitar that was similar in design to Pickett's guitar.

Judge Posner, writing for the Seventh Circuit, notes that Pickett's interpretation of the law creates an impossible situation: "Whether Prince's guitar is a copy of his own copyrighted symbol or a copy of Pickett's guitar is likewise not a question that the methods of litigation can readily answer. If anyone can make derivative works based on the Prince symbol, we could have hundreds of Picketts, each charging infringement by others." And, we might add, each charging infringement by Prince.

Posner finds Pickett's theory to be implausible and contrary to correct interpretation of the Copyright statute. Pickett overlooks the implication of Section 106(2) of the Copyright Act which grants the owner of a copyright the exclusive right to prepare derivative works based upon the copyrighted work.[4] As a result, "Pickett could not make a derivative work based on the Prince symbol without Prince's authorization even if Pickett's guitar had a smidgen of originality."

Section 103(b) should not be read as qualifying the exclusive right of the copyright holder to make derivative works. The creator of a derivative work is not permitted incorporate material that infringes another's copyright. Pickett had no right to create the derivative work in the first place, and therefore could secure no rights in the result. "[T]he only copyright that Pickett claims Prince infringed is a copyright that Pickett had no right to obtain, namely a copyright on a derivative work based on Prince's copyrighted symbol."

Confusion on this point can be traced back to the Second Circuit's decision in *Eden Toys, Inc. v. Florelee Undergarment Co.*, where the court indicated that a person can make a derivative work without the permission of the owner of the copyright in the original work if the original work does not "pervade" the derivative work.[5] The notion that it is possible to create a derivative work in which the original is not pervasive arises from confusion about the meaning of a derivative work. The language in *Eden* defines "derivative work" too broadly. It is more appropriate to distinguish derivative works, where the original is pervasive, from works only loosely connected with the original, where the original is not pervasive. The latter category should not be deemed "derivative" works at all within the meaning of the statute.

Judge Posner's interpretation of the statute aligns with common sense and provides a clearer understand of derivative works than may have been the case based on past decisions. Simply put, the lesson of the *Prince* case seems to be that a stranger to the rights in the original work may not establish rights in a derivative work, but may create rights in a work "loosely based" on a prior work if it is sufficiently different from the original so that it would not be deemed a derivative work. In the end, it becomes a matter of common sense: did the second party infringe the original work, or not.

11

THE LIMITATION PERIOD FOR COPYRIGHT CLAIMS

She who hesitates is lost. Such is the lesson of *Maurizio v. Goldsmith*, a decision that merits consideration by those seeking to avoid the pitfalls of the limitations on copyright actions.[1]

Cynthia Maurizio claimed that she collaborated with Olivia Goldsmith on a book outline and two draft chapters for *The First Wives Club*, a novel that ultimately became a best-seller and a popular motion picture. In 1990, Goldsmith submitted that outline and completed the book for publication. On January 23, 1991, Maurizio learned that the movie rights to *The First Wives Club* had been sold.

Maurizio then filed an action in state court for breach of contract, fraudulent inducement, conversion and unjust enrichment. On June 21, 1994, the state court dismissed Maurizio's complaint because the claims were preempted by the Copyright Act. On December 14, 1995, the state appellate court affirmed the dismissal.

In June, 1996, Maurizio filed a complaint in federal court for copyright infringement and a declaration of joint authorship, along with other state law claims. The district court dismissed these claims based on the three-year statute of limitations in the Copyright Act, and Maurizio appealed.

The starting point for the appellate decision is the Copyright Act. Section 507(b) of the Copyright Act provides that a copyright action must be commenced within three years after the claim accrues.[2] Thus, claims against the acts of infringement occurring more than three years prior to the filing of the complaint were properly barred. Moreover, the claim for joint authorship was also barred because it was first asserted more than three years after Maurizio first learned of the sale of the movie rights.

In an attempt to overcome the strict application of the statute of limitations, Maurizio sought to apply the doctrine of equitable tolling on the grounds that her claims were timely filed in the wrong forum. This doctrine applies when the same statutory claim is asserted in a different forum. For example, in *Burnett v. New York Cent. R. R. Co.*, the Supreme Court held that the statute of limitations for a FELA action was tolled by a timely filed prior action that was dismissed for improper venue.[3] However, the doctrine does not apply when the claims are different.[4]

Although arising from the same facts, Maurizio's claims in the state court action were different from the claims later filed in federal court. The Court of Appeals explained the significance of this:

> Maurizio's argument misconceives the nature of the state proceedings in this case, however. Maurizio did not assert copyright claims in the state forum. She asserted a contract claim and other state causes of action in state court; and those claims were dismissed because they were preempted by Maurizio's independent federal claims under the Copyright Act. We therefore conclude that Maurizio cannot rely upon this Court's precedent applying the doctrine of equitable tolling in cases where the causes of action asserted in one court belonged in another.

The doctrine of equitable tolling may be available if the plaintiff is fraudulently induced by the defendant to delay legal action until it is too late. However, fraudulent inducement does not save claims that were not filed where a publisher advises an author that he has no valid copyright claims.[5] Reliance on another's attorney is unreasonable when the parties have adverse interests in the outcome of the advice. An independent opinion should be sought.

Maurizio could not reasonably claim to have been misled since Goldsmith's attorney raised the preemption issue well before that statute of limitations had run. Thus, Maurizio was appraised of the issue and could have filed the copyright claims in time. As explained by the Court of Appeals:

> We need not consider whether any equitable principle would have been implicated if adversary counsel in the state litigation had appreciated the preemption issue prior to the running of the statute of limitations and for tactical reasons failed to raise it until after the statute had run. In this case, Goldsmith's lawyer argued from the outset that Maurizio's state law claims were preempted by the Copyright Act, and that the dispute belonged in federal court. There was therefore no attempt by adversary counsel to render Maur-

izio complacent in the wrong forum until the statute of limitations for her federal claims expired.

Given this warning, Maurizio's failure to pursue copyright claims is puzzling.
Whatever the reason, the consequence is serious: the loss of copyright infringement and joint authorship claims.

The doctrine of continuous infringement may also affect the application of
the statute of limitations on copyright actions. Where there is an ongoing
infringement involving a single infringing work, some courts have tolled the statute of limitations period, allowing an action brought within three years of the last
act of infringement to reach back to allow relief for conduct occurring more than
three years prior to suit.[6] In these cases, the initial copying was not deemed to be
a separate and complete wrong. Rather, it was simply the first step in course of
wrongful conduct.

The continuous infringement doctrine has been criticized and may now be
unavailable in some circuits.[7] Where the doctrine is not followed, recovery will
only be allowed for acts occurring within the three-year limitations period. So,
for example, if the act of copying occurred five years ago, but the infringing work
continues to be distributed, the copyright owner would be able to recover for the
unauthorized distribution during the past three years, but not for the initial copying or first two years of distribution. Thus, in Maurizio's case, she was permitted
to pursue copyright infringement claims that involved recent acts of infringement.

12

THE FIRST SALE DOCTRINE

In recent years, the U.S. Supreme Court has devoted an unusually high level of attention to copyright matters, deciding two case in the first quarter of 1998 with important effects on litigation strategy.

In *Quality King Distributors, Inc. v. L'anza Research International, Inc.*, the Supreme Court addressed the impact of the first sale doctrine on the ability to prevent parallel imports under Section 602 of the Copyright Act of 1976.[1]

L'anza is a manufacturer of heavily advertised hair care products sold in the United States through limited and exclusive distribution channels. In foreign markets, however, L'anza's advertising activities are minimal and it sells its products at a lower price. As a result, Quality King acquired L'anza's products abroad and resold them at discounted prices in the United States. L'anza objected to Quality King's importation of products bearing L'anza's copyrighted labels as a violation of Lanza's right under Section 602 of the Copyright Act to prevent the unauthorized importation of copies.[2]

Quality King claimed that L'anza's rights under Section 602 of the Copyright Act were limited by the "first sale" doctrine in Section 109(a), which permits the owner of a lawful copy to resell that copy without violating the rights of the copyright holder.[3]

The District Court and Ninth Circuit agreed with L'anza, concluding that the right to prevent unauthorized importation of copies would be meaningless if the first sale doctrine was a defense.

The Supreme Court had a different view. Section 602 provides that importation "is an infringement of the exclusive right to distribute…under Section 106." Section 106, in turn expressly states that all of the exclusive copyrights, including the right to distribute, are limited by Sections 107 through 120. One of the limitations provided by Section 109(a) is the ability of the owner of a lawfully made copy to sell that copy without violating the exclusive right of distribution.

Accordingly, Justice Stevens concluded that the first sale doctrine is applicable to imported copies that were lawfully made under the Act and acquired abroad.

Justice Stevens, noted that the court's conclusion did not render Section 602(a) meaningless. The importation clause still provides a private action against the importer of copies that were "lawfully made" under another's country's law, but not under U.S. law.

The problem of parallel imports has nagged U.S. manufacturers for decades.[4] The use of the trademark laws to prevent such importation is complicated by findings that parallel imports are genuine goods and as a consequence cannot create a likelihood of confusion.[5] As a result, litigators have turned from the trademark laws to Section 602 of the Copyright Law as a simple and easy way to prevent parallel imports into the U.S.[6] After *L'anza*, this strategy is no longer available since parallel imports will, by definition, involve goods lawfully made by the copyright owner.

What protection remains? Parallel imports can still be prevented, but it takes planning. If goods intended for sale abroad are materially different from their domestic counterparts, confusion is likely and relief will be available under U.S. Trademark Law.[7] The differences required are not great, but they must be sufficient so that confusion between the domestic and foreign product is likely. The successful plaintiff seeking to prevent parallel imports must now begin with a product design and marketing strategy that permits the litigators to present a strong case under the Trademark Laws.

13

THREATS OF LITIGATION

Clients and attorneys often want to enhance the recognition of their rights and reputation for enforcement through out of court publicity. Copyright litigators should recognize, however, that threats of litigation and press releases can give rise to counterclaims. Recent decisions outside the copyright arena provide guidelines on how far you can go.

Imagine you have filed suit against a web site operator who republishes your client's copyrighted fashion photographs. Other infringers dot the Internet, so your client wants to send warning letters to potential defendants and press releases about the case to industry publications. What are the risks? Should you intervene to control or prevent this campaign?

There is certainly cause for concern. In one instance, for example, Hewlett-Packard filed counterclaims for contractual interference, unfair competition and injurious falsehood against Computer Aid, Inc. and its attorneys for statements made in a press release about the initial lawsuit. The district court judge in Philadelphia ruled that the jury should decide the claims.[1]

WHAT ARE THE GUIDELINES?

The Tenth Circuit case of *Cardtoons, L.C. v. Major League Baseball Players Association* is instructive.[2] The case involved parody trading cards made by Cardtoons and printed by Champs Marketing. The defendant sent cease and desist letters to both, alleging a violation of the player's right of publicity. Relying on the First Amendment, Cardtoons prevailed in its declaratory judgment action, then pressed claims for tortuous interference based on the letter to Champs. The court found that the cease and desist letters were immune from action because of the *Noerr-Pennington* doctrine.

Originating as a rule in anti-trust cases, the *Noerr-Pennington* doctrine now transcends its roots. The doctrine provides immunity from any liability arising out of a party's filing and maintaining any civil lawsuit and can be overcome only upon a showing that the lawsuit is a mere "sham," i.e. both (1) objectively baseless and (2) intended as an anti-competitive weapon.[3]

In *Cardtoons*, the court held that warnings about litigation "enjoy the same level of protection from liability as litigation itself"and stated:

> We hold that a Defendant...who has probable cause to threaten litigation and makes no assertion beyond the legal and factual bases for the threats, may enjoy Noerr-Pennington immunity from a claim of libel...The statements that Cardtoons labels as libelous are coextensive with the threats of litigation to which we have already attached Noerr-Pennington immunity. If Cardtoon's argument prevails, a Defendant would be exposed to libel claims even if his litigation or threat to litigate were supported by probable cause. By allowing an alternative cause of action against petitions that are otherwise eligible for immunity, the argument renders Noerr-Pennington a nullity.

The privilege has also been extended to post-filing publicity about a lawsuit. In *Aircapital Cablevision, Inc. v. Starlink Communications Group*, plaintiff Multimedia issued press releases and threatened suits against customers of defendant Starlink.[4] The press releases implied that Starlink customers were "pirates" and were "stealing" from cable companies. Although the law suit and publicity caused Starlink to lose business and customers, and Multimedia admittedly hoped to put Starlink out of business, the court found no liability as a matter of law:

> Clearly, Multimedia was engaging in bully-type conduct and undoubtedly Starlink's business was hurt as a result. Although Multimedia would have been better advised to have refrained from making such comments, this short-lived publicity and its indirect threats against Starlink's customers were incidental to the lawsuit. Therefore, the publicity is also protected by the Noerr-Pennington doctrine.

Other cases have similarly recognized that publicity relating to a lawsuit is entitled to the Noerr-Pennington immunity.[5] Nevertheless, the conduct entails risk and counsel should carefully review any such materials to insure that all statements are accurate.

PART II
TRADEMARK

14

UNITED STATES TRADEMARK LAW IN BRIEF

The principal source of civil trademark law in the United States is the Lanham Act, a federal trademark statute that provides for the registration of trademarks and for the protection of registered and unregistered trademarks. The individual states also provide protection for trademarks by statute or common law. The federal courts have original jurisdiction over civil actions for trademark infringement arising under the federal statute. Claims may also be brought in state courts.

The principal interest of U.S. trademark law is to protect the public from deception in the marketplace. The secondary interest is to protect the trademark owner's rights in the value of the trademark as a designation of source.

The definition of a trademark under U.S. law is broad. A mark is any device that serves as an indication of source. In addition to words or logos, a trademark may be a sound, color, slogan, product configuration or smell. To serve as an indication of source, a device must be inherently distinctive (i.e., immediately recognized by consumers as a designation of source) or must acquire distinctiveness or "secondary meaning" through use (i.e., come to be recognized as an designation of source). Secondary meaning is proved through circumstantial evidence such as length and amount of use, media recognition, and survey evidence.

There are basic four classifications of trademarks: generic, descriptive, suggestive and arbitrary. Generic terms are never protected. Descriptive terms (such as names and geographic places) can be protected only after they acquire secondary meaning. Suggestive terms are protected upon use in commerce. Arbitrary terms (such as KODAK or EXXON) are deemed to be inherently distinctive and can also be protected upon use.

Trademark rights in the United States arise from use, not from registration. Registration is beneficial, however, to increase the scope of protection. For example, upon registration, the registrant receives nationwide constructive use back to

43

the date of application. After five years a registered mark may become incontestable so that it can no longer be challenged as descriptive.

The test for trademark infringement is whether the junior user's use of a mark is likely to create confusion with the senior user's use of its mark. Likelihood of confusion is determined by considering various factors including: the strength of the plaintiff's mark; the similarity of the marks; the similarity of the goods or services involved; the similarity of the channels of trade; the nature of the purchase and purchaser; evidence of actual confusion; and, the intent of the defendant. None of these factors are determinative. Infringement is not determined by an in-court side-by-side comparison of the marks, but must be based on the marks as they are encountered in the marketplace.

The strength of a mark refers to its level of distinctiveness and recognition. A highly distinctive, well-known mark is entitled to a broader scope of protection than a descriptive mark. The marks and goods need not be identical to establish infringement. The use of confusingly similar marks for related goods or services may be sufficient to create a likelihood of confusion. Evidence of actual confusion and bad intent are not required to establish infringement. The courts recognize that evidence of actual confusion is difficult to obtain. When found, however, actual confusion is deemed to be the best evidence of a likelihood of confusion. Since the test for infringement involves deception of the public, lack of bad intent is not a defense. Intent to infringe, however, will raise a presumption of a likelihood of confusion. Evidence used to prove infringement typically consists of direct testimony on the relevant factors, as well as survey evidence regarding the reaction of relevant purchasers.

Although trademark law prohibits uses that create a likelihood of confusion regarding the source of the goods, it does permit some uses. Permissible uses include parody, comparative advertising, and indications of compatibility or descriptive use.

The trademark owner initiates a claim for infringement by filing a complaint in state or federal court. (The general public does not have standing to sue for trademark infringement.) If the trademark owner seeks damages, a jury may hear the case; otherwise a judge will hear the case.

The relief available for trademark infringement includes injunctive relief, destruction of the infringing marks, and monetary damages. Monetary relief may include actual damages, lost profits, or an award of the infringer's profits. Attorney's fees may be awarded in extraordinary cases, such as cases of willful infringement. Under federal law, the awards for infringement constitute compensation, not a penalty, although punitive damages may be available under state law.

Preliminary injunctive relief for trademark infringement is available upon consideration of the following factors: likelihood of success on the merits; threat of immediate, irreparable injury; the balance of hardship between the parties; and, the public interest. Summary judgment prior to trial may be granted if there are no material disputes of fact and one party is entitled to judgment as a matter of law.

The final decision of the trial court can be appealed to the court of appeals for review of legal error or clearly erroneous findings of fact. A final appeal to the Supreme Court is possible, but is usually granted only to resolve conflicts between the lower courts over interpretation of the federal statute.

The Lanham Act also provides causes of action against trademark counterfeiting and dilution of a trademark. Counterfeiting occurs when someone uses a spurious mark that is identical with or substantially indistinguishable from a registered mark. The relief available for counterfeiting includes an *ex parte* seizure of goods and records, lost profits, punitive damages, prejudgment interest, statutory damages and attorney's fees.

Dilution statutes protect the trademark owner's interest in the value of a famous mark by providing injunctive relief against tarnishment of the mark or blurring of the distinctiveness of the mark. The fame of a mark is determined by considering various factors: the length of use; the amount of sales and advertising; public recognition; and, the absence of similar marks used by third parties. Tarnishment occurs when the defendant associates the plaintiff's mark with unsavory goods or activities. Blurring of the distinctiveness of a mark is generally found when a unique and well-known mark is used for unrelated goods or services, thereby reducing the public's association of the mark with the plaintiff. A likelihood of confusion regarding the source or sponsorship of the defendant's goods or services is not an element of a dilution claim. Protection against dilution is also available under the statutes of various states.

15

LIKELIHOOD OF CONFUSION: UNDERSTANDING TRADEMARK LAW'S KEY PRINCIPLE

Likelihood of confusion is the key term of art in trademark law. All trademark infringement cases turn on this issue. Yet the words alone hold little content. This article examines the content of phrase as provided by statute and case law, considers how that content has changed over time, and identifies some issues that may be important to the concept of confusion in the future.

BACKGROUND

In 1944, the likelihood of confusion concept entered federal statutory law. Section 32 of the Lanham Act[1] provides a cause of action against any person who shall:

> use in commerce any reproduction, counterfeit, copy, or colorable imitation of a registered mark in connection with the sale, offering for sale, distribution, or advertising of any goods or services on or in connection with which such use is likely to cause confusion, or to cause mistake, or to deceive.

Similar protection arose under Section 43(a) of the Lanham Act[2] which originally stated:

> Any person who shall affix, apply, or annex, or use in connection with any goods or services, or any container or containers for goods, a false designation of origin, or any false description or representation, including words or other symbols tending falsely to describe or represent the same, and shall cause such goods or services to enter into commerce...shall be liable to a civil action...by any person who believes that he is or is likely to be damaged by the use of such false description or representation.

Although originally not clearly encompassing the use of mark that is likely to cause confusion, Section 43(a) developed into a provision that covered infringement of unregistered marks and trade dress in effectively the same manner as Section 32 covered registered marks. With the Trademark Law Revision Act of 1987, Section 43(a)(1)(A), was revised to provide explicit protection for the likelihood of confusion consistent with the then developed case law, and now states:

> Any person who, on or in connection with any goods or services, or any container for goods, uses in commerce any word, term, name, symbol, or device, or an combination thereof...which is likely to cause confusion, or to cause mistake, or to deceive as to the affiliation, connection, or association of such person with another person, or as to the origin, sponsorship, or approval of his or her goods, services, or commercial activities by another person...shall be liable in a civil action by any such person who believes that he or she is or is likely to be damaged by such act.

With that amendment, the protection recognized by the courts for unregistered marks and trade dress became explicit. The current version of Section 43(a) provides a comprehensive standard for interpreting likelihood of confusion.

TYPES OF CONFUSION

Generally, there are three types of confusion: actual, source, and sponsorship. Actual confusion occurs when a person mistakes one product or service for that of another because of similar names or packaging. For example, persons familiar with PINE-SOL cleaner who encounter PINE-SOLL cleaner in a similar package are likely to mistake it for the national brand.

Source confusion occurs when a person believes that two products come from the same source or are manufactured by the same company. Persons familiar with the BERGHOFF restaurant in CHICAGO would not mistake BERGHOFF frozen dinners for the popular restaurant, but they are likely to believe that the frozen dinners are manufactured by the restaurant.

Sponsorship confusion occurs when a person is likely to believe that the second product is authorized, sponsored, or approved by the original company. When a person sees a CUBS logo on a baseball hat, she does not mistake the hat for a baseball team, nor does she think that the baseball team has entered into the hat business. She does, however, think that the hat is authorized or sponsored by the baseball team.

Each of these three types of confusion is actionable. In each case, the basis for trademark protection is to prevent deception of the public. The public's interest is primary; the trademark owner's interest is secondary. In other words, the trademark owner's rights are protected so that the public is not deceived, and the scope of the trademark owner's rights are (or should be) exactly equal to the scope of rights necessary to prevent deception of the public.

THE SUBJECTS AND OBJECTS OF CONFUSION

Since trademark infringement arose as a species of unfair competition, it was initially thought that the confusion could only be created by a competitor. The early cases now seem quaint, but at the time it was not so obvious that principles of unfair competition could be extended to situations where there was no competition between the parties. In 1917, for example, the Second Circuit asserted in *Aunt Jemima Mills Co. v. Rigney & Co.*,[3] where the district court had decided that use of the mark AUNT JEMIMA'S for pancake syrup did not infringe the plaintiff's rights in the same mark for flour:

> It is said that even a technical trade-mark may be appropriated by anyone in any market for goods not in competition with those of the prior user. This was the view of the court below in saying that no one wanting syrup could possible be made to take flour. But we think that goods, though different, may be so related as to fall within the mischief which equity should prevent. Syrup and flour are both food products, and food products commonly used together. Obviously the public, or a large part of it, seeing this trade-mark on a syrup, would conclude that it was made by the complainant. Perhaps they might not do so, if it were used for flatirons. In this way the complainant's reputation is put in the hands of the defendants. It will enable them to get the benefit of the complainant's reputation and advertisement. These we think are property rights which should be protected in equity.

Thus, since the early case law recognized that a broad range of goods or services can result in a likelihood of confusion, it should be no surprise when a modern tribunal finds confusion between the use of the same mark on shoes and hair care products.[4]

For similar reasons, it was also argued in early unfair competition cases that the victim of the confusion must be engaged in business, thereby excluding protection to charitable institutions. As late as 1975, this notion was still noted favorably by the First Circuit in *DeCosta v. Columbia Broadcasting System, Inc.,*[5] (denying protection on other grounds to the creator of the Paladin persona as a charitable entertainment for children):

> We hesitate to take the step of offering common law unfair competition protection to eleemosynary individuals. Whether legislatures are better equipped than courts to deal with this problem, we cannot clearly say, but in our posture of doubt would prefer to see expansion of protection come from that source.

The trademark laws are not designed to prevent all persons from being confused. Likelihood of confusion is determined on the basis of a "reasonably prudent consumer" and depends on the circumstances. When expert buyers are involved, the standard becomes the "reasonably prudent expert buyer." When children are involved, the standard is "reasonably prudent child" because the courts generally rule that children are less discerning than adults and more likely to be confused. When there are mixed buyer classes, the Third Circuit has held that "the standard of care to be exercised by the reasonably prudent purchaser will be equal to that of the least sophisticated consumer."

WHEN DOES CONFUSION OCCUR?

Initially, the only relevant confusion involved the purchase of the parties' goods. Section 32(1) of the Lanham Act only proscribed likelihood of confusion, mistake or deception of "purchasers as to the source of origin of such goods and services." In 1962, however, Congress amended the Act to delete the quoted portion from the section.[6] Now it is clear that relevant confusion can involve any person, consumer, prospective consumer, end user or even an uninvolved onlooker. The result is a much expanded confusion test encompassing non-purchasers.

Confusion that occurs *after* the initial purchase is referred to as "post-sale confusion." The injury derives in part from the fact that post-sale non-purchasers may be prospective purchasers, with the confusion potentially affecting their future purchasing decisions. As stated in *Lois Sportswear, U.S.A., Inc., v. Levi Strauss & Co.*,[7] "The confusion the Act seeks to prevent in this context is that a consumer seeing [appellant's] familiar stitching pattern will associate the jeans with appellee and that association will influence his buying decisions." Thus, even if the street corner retailer explains to a purchaser that the cheap ROLEX watch is a counterfeit, the retailer will still be liable because people who observe the purchaser wearing the counterfeit, or who receive the watch as a gift, are likely to be confused into believing it is the real thing.[8] The direct purchaser, furthermore, might sell it to an unknowing third party without explaining that it is counterfeit.

The recognition of pre-purchase confusion was slower to develop. Perhaps the earliest case was *Grotrian, Hefferich, Schulz, Th. Steinweg Nachf. v. Steinway & Sons*,[9] where the Second Circuit declined in 1975 to hold "that actual or potential confusion at the time of purchase necessarily must be demonstrated to establish trademark infringement." The court explained that the harm at issue was not that someone would be confused when she bought the piano. Rather, that harm arose because the "Grotrian-Steinweg" name would attract potential customers based on the Steinway reputation. Later, in *Mobil Oil Corp. v. Pegasus Petroleum Corp.*,[10] the Second Circuit found the defendant's use of its name would infringe Mobil's use of a flying horse logo because "potential purchasers would be misled into an initial interest" in the defendant's products, even if they learned the truth before the sale was consummated. The court therefore held that "such initial confusion works a sufficient trademark injury."

Recent decisions have embraced the notion of pre-purchase confusion by calling it "initial interest" confusion. In *Dr. Seuss Enters. v. Penguin Books USA, Inc.*, the Ninth Circuit recognized in 1997 that the use of another's trademark in a manner calculated "to capture initial consumer attention, even though no actual sale is finally completed as a result of the confusion, may be still an infringement."[11]

The question becomes, what interest is served by pre-purchase or initial interest confusion? It does not protect the public from deception because by definition, the deception is corrected by the time the public makes a purchasing decision. Instead, initial interest confusion seems to protect the trademark owner's interest in the goodwill of the mark or to prevent others from benefiting from the commercial magnetism of the mark. *Brookfield Communications, Inc. v. West Coast Entertainment* suggests that the wrong caused by initial interest confusion is the misappropriation of goodwill.[12] That concern, however, is not directly related to preventing public deception. Therefore, the recognition of pre-purchase or initial interest confusion as a basis for relief rests on a fundamentally different foundation than traditional trademark law and may prove unsound.

WHERE DOES CONFUSION OCCUR?

U.S. trademark law is unique. While U.S. law recognizes that trademark rights are territorial, confusion occurring outside the United States may be actionable under U.S. law.[13] This is a departure from the norm. The Anti-Trust laws also have extraterritorial application,[14] but most U.S. laws only apply to action within the United States. The U.S. Copyright Laws, for example, generally have no extraterritorial application.[15]

The test for extraterritorial application of the federal trademark laws involves three issues: (1) there must be some effect on American foreign commerce; (2) the effect must be sufficiently great to present at cognizable injury to plaintiffs under the federal statute; and (3) the interests of American foreign commerce must be sufficiently strong in relation to those of other nations to justify an assertion of extraterritorial authority.[16]

Most extraterritorial application cases require confusion within the U.S. In *Steele v. Bulova Watch Co.*,[17] the Supreme Court held in 1952 that the U.S. trademark laws applied when a U.S. citizen used the BULOVA mark in Mexico. In *Bulova*, there was some evidence of confusion within the U.S. because some of the watches came back into Texas. Not all extraterritorial application cases require confusion within the U.S., however. In *Reebok International, Ltd. v. Marnatech Enterprises, Inc.*,[18] the Ninth Circuit found that the U.S. trademark laws applied in a case where the actual consumer sales of the infringing products may have occurred only in Mexico. The Second Circuit held in *Vanity Fair Mills v. T. Eaton Co.* that the Lanham Act "should not be given extraterritorial application against foreign citizens acting under presumably valid trademarks in a foreign country."[19] A similar result was reached in *Totalplan Corporation of America v. Colborne*,[20] where the Second Circuit refused to apply the Lanham Act to the distribution of cameras in Japan.

HOW MUCH CONFUSION IS ENOUGH?

The United States Supreme Court has recognized that the junior user does not have an obligation to avoid all possibility of confusion. Instead, the junior user has the obligation "to use every reasonable means to prevent confusion."[21] In recent years, the Third Circuit went beyond the boundaries of that rule and held that the standard for infringement when the defendant enters a new field occupied by an established business should be the "possibility of confusion," rather that the traditional standard of likelihood of confusion.[22] It has since retreated from that position, confirming that the standard for determining trademark infringement under the Lanham Act is likelihood of confusion and cannot be lowered to a "possibility of confusion."[23] Likelihood of confusion is thus firmly established as the controlling principle for trademark infringement.

Surveys are often used to show that prospective purchasers are likely to be confused, but what percentage of confusion is sufficient to demonstrate a likelihood of confusion? In *James Burroughs, Ltd. v. Sign of the Beefeater, Inc.*,[24] the Court of Appeals for the Seventh Circuit rejected the district court's characterization of 15% confusion as "small," stating:

> We cannot agree that 15% is "small." Though the percentage of likely confusion required may vary from case to case, we cannot consider 15%, in the context of this case, involving the entire restaurant-going community, to be *de minimus*.

Thus, the court concluded that 15% confusion "evidences a likelihood of confusion, deception or mistake regarding the sponsorship of [defendant's] services sufficient on this record to establish Distiller's right to relief." In contrast, in *Henri's Food Products Co., Inc. v. Kraft, Inc.*[25] the Seventh Circuit held that the district court was correct in holding that a 7.6% confusion weighs against a finding of infringement.

Typically, survey researchers and courts recognize that survey results include a "noise" level (or level of meaningless responses) of about 5%. Accordingly, a level of confusion below 10% is at risk of being dismissed as *de minimus*, while 15% to 20% or more is usually deemed to be solid evidence in support of a finding of likelihood of confusion.

WHAT FACTORS ARE CONSIDERED?

All of the federal courts apply multi-factor tests as guidelines in assessing the likelihood of confusion occurring. One of the first to set forth such a test was the Second Circuit in *Polaroid Corp. v. Polarad Electronics Corp.*, in 1961:[26]

> Where the products are different, the prior owner's chance of success is a function of many variables: the strength of his mark, the degree of similarity between the two marks, the proximity of the products, the likelihood that the

prior owner will bridge the gap, actual confusion, and the reciprocal of defendant's good faith in adopting its own mark, the quality of defendant's product, and the sophistication of the buyers. Even this extensive catalogue does not exhaust the possibilities—the court may have to take still other variables into account.

The Second Circuit now applies that test in competing goods cases as well.[27]

The other circuits utilize similar factor tests: for example, the First Circuit, *Boston Athletic Ass'n. v. Sullivan;*[28] the Third Circuit, *Ford Motor Co. v Summit Motor Products, Inc.,*[29] (listing ten relevant factors); the Seventh Circuit, *Schwinn Bicycle Co. v. Ross Bicycles, Inc.*[30] (referring to the factors as "digits" of confusion); and the Eleventh Circuit, *ConAgra, Inc. v. Singleton.*[31] Some courts use the factors listed in Section 729 of the Restatement of Torts (1938), for example, the Tenth Circuit, *Beer Nuts, Inc. v. Clover Club Foods Co.*[32] Perhaps the most comprehensive list of factors appears in the 1973 case, *In re E. I. Du Pont de Nemours & Co.:*[33]

1. The similarity or dissimilarity of the marks in their entireties as to appearance, sound, connotation and commercial impression.

2. The similarity or dissimilarity and nature of the goods or services as described in an application or registration or in connection with which a prior mark is in use.

3. The similarity or dissimilarity of established, likely-to-continue trade channels.

4. The conditions under which and buyers to whom sales are made, i.e. "impulse" vs. careful, sophisticated purchasing.

5. The fame of the prior mark (sales, advertising, length of use).

6. The number and nature of similar marks in use on similar goods.

7. The nature and extent of any actual confusion.

8. The length of time during and conditions under which there has been concurrent use without evidence of actual confusion.

9. The variety of goods on which a mark is or is not used (house mark, "family" mark, product mark).

10. The market interface between applicant and the owner of a prior mark:

    a. a mere "consent" to register or use.

b. agreement provisions designed to preclude confusion, i.e. limitations on continued use of the marks by each party.

c. assignment of mark, application, registration and good will of the related business.

d. laches and estoppel attributable to owner of prior mark and indicative of lack of confusion.

11. The extent to which applicant has a right to exclude others from use of its mark on its goods.

12. The extent of potential confusion, i.e., whether *de minimis* or substantial.

13. Any other established fact probative of the effect of use.

The *Du Pont* factors continue to provide a useful and comprehensive checklist for proof of likelihood of confusion.

It must be remembered that the factor tests are only aids in determining the ultimate issue of likelihood of confusion. The analysis of confusion is a question of fact, not a mechanical process or calculation. There is no precise mathematical formula. The factor tests are helpful guidelines, not "hoops a district court need jump through." It is erroneous to engage in a "pedantic" application of the factors without consideration of the totality of circumstances. Ultimately, we are concerned only about whether in fact the public will be deceived by the defendant's conduct.

WHAT'S NEXT?

A principal characteristic of the past century of law involving likelihood of confusion has been the ever expanding scope of protection afforded to trademark owners at the expense of competitors and other persons who use names or symbols that remind the court of another's mark. The scope of protection has expanded in terms of what is recognized as a mark, the relationship of the goods and services, the uses involved and the circumstances when the junior user's mark is encountered. Other indications of this trend have been the incorporation of dilution law into the federal statute,[34] and the protection of trademarks against the registration of similar domain names[35] where protection can be granted without consideration of a likelihood of confusion between the use of the parties' marks.

Overall, this protection has benefited the public by reducing consumer deception and has helped in the efficient exchange of information in the market place.

It must be recalled, however, that trademark rights are not rights in gross. As stated by Judge Posner in *Illinois High School Association v. GTE Vantage, Inc.,*[36] "What matters is that a trademark is not nearly so secure an entitlement as a property right. It is mainly just a designation of source." The United States Supreme Court has long acknowledged the limits to the scope protection that should be afforded trademark rights, recognizing a right to share in another's goodwill when there is no evidence of passing off or deception. In 1938, while denying claims of exclusive rights in the name and in the pillow-shaped biscuit configuration of SHREDDED WHEAT, the Supreme Court stated in *Kellogg Co. v. National Biscuit Co.*:[37]

> [The defendant] Kellogg Company is undoubtedly sharing in the goodwill of the article known as "Shredded Wheat"; and thus is sharing in a market which was created by the skill and judgment of plaintiff's predecessor and has been widely extended by vast expenditures in advertising persistently made. But that is not unfair. Sharing in the goodwill of an article unprotected by patent or trade-mark is the exercise of a rights possessed by all and in the free exercise of which the consuming public is deeply interested.

As the law involving likelihood of confusion moves forward in the next century, we can anticipate a tension between the right to protect trademark rights and the conflicting right to share in another's goodwill when there is no deception. We should not hope for an expansion of trademark rights into a right in gross, for that limits the choices available in the market while failing to further the interests of the public in avoiding confusion. We can hope that the courts will establish rational and consistent limits on trademark rights that fully protect the legitimate interests of owners, competitors and the public. The touchstone for achieving that goal is the sound application of the likelihood of confusion principle.

16

TRADE DRESS PROTECTION AND THE PROBLEM OF DISTINCTIVENESS

The problem of trade dress protection is this: what rules should we apply to trade dress protection to best satisfy the goals of trademark law? The merit of various proposed solutions can be measured by evaluating how effective they are in achieving those goals in various disputes.

Trademark law is directed toward three general goals: (1) protection of the public from confusion, mistake and deception;[1] (2) protection of the trademark owner's goodwill;[2] and (3) prevention of unfair acts by others.[3] These goals are inter-related, with the primary goal being the protection of the public.[4] That primary goal is the basis for understanding the meaning of the other goals. To understand the other two goals we must consider them in the context of public perception. Otherwise, the other two goals become abstractions, with no coherent meaning.

The identity of a trademark owner's goodwill is determined by public perception.[5] It is the collection of favorable associations found in the public mind. Goodwill is damaged when those favorable associations of the public are damaged. Likewise, in the trademark context, whether an act affecting the business of another is unfair depends on its effect on the public mind.

As an example, suppose that Armstrong Corporation adopts the name AMAZE for widgets. The Brewster Company later adopts AMAZE for gadgets. Armstrong cries that this is an unfair act. But is it? The mere fact that the names are the same means nothing. The answer depends on the public mind. Does the public associate the name AMAZE with Armstrong? When the public encounters Brewster's use of AMAZE, is it confused or deceived?

The answers to these questions turn on an analysis of the two basic issues of trademark law—distinctiveness and likelihood of confusion. Rephrasing the questions using those terms of art, we must first decide if AMAZE is distinctive, meaning that the public associates the name used in connection with widgets with a single source. If so, then we must decide if there is a likelihood of confusion—that is, whether the relevant public is likely to experience confusion, mistake or deception due to Brewster's use of AMAZE.

Both issues should be understood from the perspective of the relevant public, not from that of the court, the trademark owner or the infringer. The questions we seek to answer only have coherent meaning if we consider the perception of the public. Otherwise, we are unable to determine if the plaintiff has any goodwill to protect or if the defendant's acts are unfair. When the results or reasoning of a trademark or trade dress decision seem flawed or confused, the cause often lies in a failure to analyze the problem based on the perception of the public.

This article will focus on the distinctiveness analysis for trade dress protection. The article begins with a review of the fundamental principles arising in early decisions, and it then turns to the development of categories as a tool for the distinctiveness analysis. Next, the article addresses the problems in the application of that analysis, and it discusses the resolution offered by the Supreme Court in *Two Pesos, Inc. v. Taco Cabana, Inc.*[6] and *Wal-Mart Stores, Inc. v. Samara Brothers, Inc.*[7] Finally, the article considers how well that resolution addresses the problem of trade dress protection.

TRADE DRESS DEFINED

Trade dress has been defined by the Supreme Court as "the total image of a product[,] and may include features such as size, shape, color or color combinations, texture, graphics, or even particular sales techniques."[8] It includes "the shape and design of the product itself."[9] It can be viewed as any aspect of overall appearance that "act[s] as a symbol that distinguishes a firm's goods and identifies their source, without serving any other significant function."[10]

HISTORICAL BACKGROUND

The concepts surrounding distinctiveness began to emerge in the case law of the early twentieth century. In 1917, for example, the Sixth Circuit considered a trade dress infringement case involving the packaging for fly paper.[11] The case is significant for its recognition of the rationale for such protection:

Wherever, then, the first user has through a particular trade dress, as here, *so identified his product as to indicate that it is his*, every principle of fair dealing, fair competition, forbids any subsequent user of the same product to adopt any part of the first user's dress without otherwise effectively distinguishing his dress from that of the first user.

How are we to know when a plaintiff has "so identified" his product so as to earn protection? It is through the combination of "details for the very purpose of denoting the origin of his product." Those details may be unremarkable when segregated, but when aggregated, they create trade dress that identifies the product as his. "[I]t is through such distinctive characteristics, considered in a unitary way, that the first user and the public can be protected against confusion and deception as to his product."

In this language, we see the beginning of the principle that "distinctive" trade dress may serve to identify the source of the product. The perspective of the consumer is implied, but not directly identified. The public's perception appears more clearly in the language of a 1933 case involving the mark DOBBS for hats.[12] The court notes that efforts to distinguish one mark from another in the marketplace "will largely depend upon the connotations which the public has become habituated to attach to the plaintiff's use of the name." The name has come to mean more than just a name; it has taken on a new meaning:

Since this name *has acquired its secondary meaning* largely by advertising, that fact and the content of such advertising will indicate the association of ideas which attaches in the public mind to the name.

The defendant's mark is an infringement because it evoked "[p]recisely the same images" in the public mind as the plaintiff's.

How do we decide if the trade dress or trademark is distinctive? In 1925, a case arose over the use of the mark GOLD MEDAL for flour.[13] The court recognizes that the right to protection may vary according to the type of mark:

To take another view of the matter, the degree of exclusiveness of appropriation accorded to the originator of a trade-name often varies with the kind of name he originates. If the name or mark be truly arbitrary, strange, and fanciful, it is more specially and peculiarly significant and suggestive of one man's goods, than when it is frequently used by many and in many differing kinds of business…The phrase "Gold Medal" is distinctly not in the same class of original, arbitrary, or fanciful words as "Kodak" and "Aunt Jemima." It is a laudatory phrase, suggestive of merit, recognized by some organization of authority awarding a prize. It is only allied to some particular business or person by insistent, persistent advertising.

The court is identifying an important distinction in trademark law that has become more sharply cleaved over time—the distinction between terms that are inherently distinctive—that is, terms that immediately identify source—and terms that are not, and only acquire distinctiveness through advertising or other persistent use. In other words, they acquire a "secondary meaning."

The implication of these early cases and others like them is that mere adoption and use of a device is not enough. One's mere attempt to identify one's product as his own is not sufficient in itself. The evidence should show that the attempt successfully makes that impression on the public mind. Justice Frankfurter commented on this "psychological function" of trademarks in 1942, stating: "Whatever the means employed, the aim is the same—to convey through the mark, in the minds of potential customers, the desirability of the commodity upon which it appears. Once this is attained, the trade-mark owner has something of value."[14]

An important corollary is also suggested by Justice Frankfurter's language. If the mark or trade dress conveys nothing to the public mind, the owner has nothing of value. A device may perhaps serve as an indication of source in the public mind immediately, because the device is "original, arbitrary, or fanciful," or it may only do so after "insistent, persistent advertising." The important issue is the factual question of the effect of the device on the public mind. Over time, however, there has been a tendency to shift attention from that important issue and instead focus on whether the device fits into one analytical category or the other.

THE LOVE OF CATEGORIES

The Second Circuit provided the classic statement on the categories of distinctiveness in a case involving the mark SAFARI for clothing.[15] The court stated:

> The cases, and in some instances the Lanham Act, identify four different categories of terms with respect to trademark protection. Arrayed in an ascending order which roughly reflects their eligibility to trademark status and the degree of protection accorded, these classes are (1) generic, (2) descriptive, (3) suggestive, and (4) arbitrary or fanciful.

In the lengthy explanation that follows in the case, there is little mention of the relationship of the categories to the perspective of the public. The public is given a passing nod in mentioning that a generic term cannot be protected regardless of "what success it has achieved in securing public identification." The case leaves the impression that the critical question is the identification of the correct category. If that holy grail is known, all else is revealed.

The Fifth Circuit did a better job of connecting the test to the public mind in *Chevron Chemical Co. v. Voluntary Purchasing Groups, Inc.*,[16] the leading case on the application of the categories of distinctiveness to trade dress. Deciding a dispute over the trade dress for agricultural chemicals, the court recognizes the public's place in the equation, stating:

> The purpose of a trademark is to enable consumers to distinguish between similar goods or services supplied from different sources. Some words and phrases are patently distinctive and, therefore, qualify facially for legal protection…However, descriptive terms, geographical place names, and family surnames are not inherently distinctive and do not alone identify any particular company's product. They were not protected as trademarks unless they had acquired distinctiveness through extensive use by a single supplier, *so that the public would recognize them as identifying the source of the product*. This consumer identification is known as "secondary meaning."

Acknowledging that trademark law requires a showing of secondary meaning "only when the claimed trademark is not sufficiently distinctive of itself to identify the producer," the court concludes that "[t]he same principles should apply to the protection of trade dress." Therefore, trade dress that is sufficiently distinctive in itself would be protectable without a showing of secondary meaning. This condition is met if the features at issue were arbitrarily selected and served no function either to describe the product or assist in its effective packaging.

The beginning of the lost connection between distinctiveness and the public mind is present in the *Chevron* case. If trade dress can be categorized as a "collection of arbitrary features," then it can be protected without the need to consider the effect of those arbitrary features on the public. But why is it necessarily true that arbitrary features should be protected without more? The *Chevron* case suggests a basis for decision closer to the real issue—whether the trade dress is sufficiently distinctive of itself to identify the producer. That question focuses on the perception of the public, not on the placement of the device at issue into categories.

TWO PESOS

The *Chevron* case provided a framework for analysis that was adopted by many of the circuits.[17] Following the *Chevron* analysis, trade dress that is sufficiently distinctive of itself to identify the producer may be considered inherently distinctive and entitled to protection without a showing of acquired distinctiveness. An example of such trade dress is the package in the *Chevron* case consisting of a combination of colors, geometric designs and lettering styles that create a "distinctive visual impression." A type of trade dress that would not meet that test would be packaging that serves as a description of the product. Such trade dress would not of itself identify the producer, but it might acquire distinctiveness, or secondary meaning, through use so that the public would recognize the trade dress as identifying the source of the producer.

In *Two Pesos, Inc. v. Taco Cabana, Inc.*,[18] the Supreme Court considered the protection of trade dress in the décor of Mexican restaurants. The case arose from a special verdict after a jury trial in which the jury found that the plaintiff's trade dress was inherently distinctive but lacked secondary meaning. The jury's findings in *Two Pesos* were consistent with the Fifth Circuit precedent of *Chevron*, holding that trade dress could be protected without secondary meaning if it was inherently distinctive. The finding was inconsistent, however, with precedent from other circuits that protected trade dress only where secondary meaning is shown.[19] To some observers, the jury verdict in *Two Pesos* seemed hopelessly confused. Because secondary meaning means acquired distinctiveness, how could the trade dress be distinctive and not distinctive at the same time?

The Supreme Court granted certiorari to consider whether inherently distinctive trade dress was protectable without the necessity of showing secondary meaning. The trade dress at issue was defined as:

> a festive eating atmosphere having interior dining and patio areas decorated with artifacts, bright colors, paintings and murals. The patio includes interior and exterior areas with the interior patio capable of being sealed off from the outside patio by overhead garage doors. The stepped exterior of the building is a festive and vivid color scheme using top border paint and neon stripes. Bright awnings and umbrellas continue the theme.

The Supreme Court endorsed the categories of descriptiveness set out in *Abercrombie*. Finding no basis in the Lanham Act for treating trade dress any differently from trademark, the Court held that inherently distinctive trade dress was entitled to protection without a showing of secondary meaning:

The Fifth Circuit was quite right in *Chevron*, and in this case, to follow the *Abercrombie* classifications consistently and to inquire whether trade dress for which protection is claimed under § 43(a) is inherently distinctive. If it is, it is capable of identifying products or services as coming from a specific source and secondary meaning is not required. This is the rule generally applicable to trademarks, and the protection of trademarks and trade dress under § 43(a) serves the same statutory purpose of preventing deception and unfair competition. There is no persuasive reason to apply different analysis to the two.

The Court's decision in *Two Pesos* confirms the general rule for distinctiveness and establishes that the rule applies to trade dress as well as trademarks.

APPLICATION OF *TWO PESOS*

Two Pesos left the courts to struggle to create tests and factors to determine when trade dress is inherently distinctive. The general rule is: "An identifying mark is distinctive and capable of being protected if it *either* (1) is inherently distinctive *or* (2) has acquired distinctiveness through secondary meaning." "Distinctiveness" refers to the mark's capability to distinguish the applicant's goods from those of others. Marks that serve to identify a particular source of a product because of "their intrinsic nature" are deemed "inherently distinctive." Marks that do not inherently identify a particular source may acquire distinctiveness. Since these principles apply equally to trade dress, it follows that trade dress that identifies a particular source of product because of its intrinsic nature should also be deemed "inherently distinctive" and entitled to protection without a showing of secondary meaning.

How are we to determine if trade dress is inherently distinctive? This question was not at issue in *Two Pesos*. However, with its implicit endorsement of the views stated in *Chevron*, the Court seems to support the view that trade dress should be categorized the same way as trademarks were in *Abercrombie*. In other words, if the trade dress can be categorized as suggestive, arbitrary or fanciful, then it should be considered inherently distinctive. But what do these categories mean with respect to trade dress? On that point, *Two Pesos* provides little help.

After *Two Pesos*, some of the circuits turned to *Abercrombie* and *Chevron*. For example, in 1998, the Fifth Circuit transferred the *Abercrombie* categories in full in *Pebble Beach Co. v. Tour 18 I Ltd.*[20] The case involves the protection of golf hole designs. The *Pebble Beach* decision recognizes that "[t]rademarks and trade dress are distinctive and protectable [sic] if they serve as indicators of source." Trademarks and trade dress can be classified according to the categories stated in

Abercrombie. Those that are suggestive, arbitrary, and fanciful are inherently distinctive, and require no showing of secondary meaning, "because their intrinsic nature serves to identify a particular source of product." Thus, the court connects the categories with the public mind.

The application of the test in *Pebble Beach* is instructive:

> Arbitrary and fanciful marks or trade dress bear no relationship to the products or services to which they are applied. The trade dress of Pebble Beach and Pinehurst's golf holes is a configuration of commonplace features of a golf hole and therefore does bear a relationship to the product, a golf hole. A suggestive mark or trade dress suggests, rather than describes, some particular characteristic of the goods or services to which it applies and requires the consumer to exercise the imagination in order to draw a conclusion as to the nature of the goods and services. The configurations of the features in Pebble Beach and Pinehurst's golf-hole designs create golf holes and nothing more. They require no exercise of one's imagination to realize that one is viewing a golf hole.[21]

Given that the golf holes are not arbitrary, fanciful or suggestive, they are not inherently distinctive. The application of the test now seems several steps removed from the point of the descriptiveness requirement—whether the device in questions serves to identify source. Instead, the inquiry is focusing on whether a golf hole "bear[s] a relationship to...a golf hole." The question almost seems silly. Regrettably, we become sidetracked by the application of the test—by our effort to categorize—and lose sight of the real issue.

In *Stuart Hall Co. v. Ampad Corp.*,[22] another case following *Abercrombie* and *Chevron*, the connection between the test and the real issue seems even more attenuated:

> These definitions address the relation between the product and the trade dress, *not the relation between the trade dress and the consumer.* The question they present is whether, and how much, the trade dress is dictated by the nature of the product, *not whether...consumers associate the design with its source.*

The court is arguing against a test for inherent distinctiveness adopted by the lower court that required a showing that the trade dress was "striking and memorable." Unfortunately, the reasoning used creates further separation between the public mind and the protection of trade dress, taking us to the point where trade dress is protected if it "is only tenuously connected with the nature of the product." That test bears little, if any, relationship to whether the public will react to the trade dress as an indication of source.

Finding the *Abercrombie* and *Chevron* analysis inadequate, other circuits have relied on *Seabrook Foods, Inc. v. Bar-Well Foods Ltd.*,[23] an early attempt to establish factors for determining when trade dress is inherently distinctive.[24] In *Seabrook Foods*, the Court of Customs and Patent Appeals[25] identified the following factors for inherent distinctiveness: (1) whether the design is a "'common' basic shape or design"; (2) whether the design is "unique or unusual in a particular field"; (3) whether the design is "a mere refinement of a commonly-adopted and well-known form of ornamentation for a particular class of goods"; and (4) whether it is "capable of creating a commercial impression distinct from the accompanying words."

The Third Circuit adopted yet another test for determining distinctiveness of product configuration trade dress in *Duraco Products, Inc. v. Joy Plastic Enterprises, Ltd.*[26] The court in *Duraco* finds that the classification of product-configuration trade dress as distinctive remains an open issue after *Two Pesos*:

> Because the Supreme Court in *Two Pesos* did not decide the question whether trade dress, and in particular trade dress in a product configuration, can actually ever be considered inherently distinctive—for purposes of that case, the Court assumed that the restaurant decor at issue was so—we must first embark on a journey to delineate when, if ever, product configurations should be deemed inherently distinctive.

The Third Circuit rejects the *Abercrombie* taxonomy: "[W]e do not think it helpful or proper to transplant the categorical distinctiveness inquiry developed for trademarks to product configurations, where the alleged trade dress lies in the very product itself." This is so because the product configuration is the thing itself: "Being constitutive of the product itself and thus having no such dialectical relationship to the product, the product's configuration cannot be said to be 'suggestive' or 'descriptive'…or…'fanciful'…"

According to the *Duraco* decision, product-configuration trade dress is inherently distinctive only where there is:

> a high probability that a product configuration serves a virtually exclusively identifying function for consumers—where the concerns over "theft" of an identifying feature or combination or arrangement of features and the cost to an enterprise of gaining and proving secondary meaning outweigh concerns over inhibiting competition, and where consumers are especially likely to perceive a connection between the product's configuration and its source.

Under the *Duraco* test, a product configuration trade dress may be deemed inherently distinctive if it is: (1) "unusual and memorable"; (2) "conceptually separable from the product"; and (3) "likely to serve primarily as a designator of origin of the product."

The case law developed after *Two Pesos* leaves many problems unresolved. First, there are significant differences between the circuits as to the choice and application of the tests for determining inherent distinctiveness. Thus, it is very difficult to predict results from one circuit to another, or even from one court to another. Second, some of the circuits apply different tests to package trade dress as opposed to product-configuration trade dress. What justification is there for different treatment? Finally, if trade dress is subject to the same test as trademarks for determining inherent distinctiveness, how does one determine if a trade dress is "arbitrary," "suggestive," or "merely descriptive"? These categories have relatively well-settled meaning when it comes to word marks, but what do the categories mean when applied to trade dress?

WAL-MART

In 2000, the Supreme Court turned again to the question of distinctiveness, this time involving the trade dress consisting of the overall appearance of a children's seersucker outfit in *Wal-Mart Stores, Inc. v. Samara Brothers, Inc.*[27]

The Samara Brothers claimed trade dress rights in the overall appearance of its outfits and sued Wal-Mart for the sale of imitations. The jury found in favor of the Samara Brothers and awarded damages of about $1.6 million. The district court denied Wal-Mart's motion for judgment as a matter of law, and the Second Circuit affirmed. Both courts concluded that inherently distinctive product configuration was entitled to protection without a showing of secondary meaning.

The Supreme Court called upon the parties to address the standards for making that determination. The Samara Brothers argued that the lower-court decisions were consistent with *Two Pesos* in holding that inherently distinctive trade dress was entitled to protection without showing secondary meaning. However, the Court went in a different direction, holding that product configuration could only be deemed distinctive upon a showing of secondary meaning.

The Court recognized that the distinction between inherently distinctive marks and marks that require secondary meaning has solid foundation in the Lanham Act. Although the *Two Pesos* decision confirms that there is no reason to limit that distinction only to trademarks, there is also no reason to assume that every category of thing eligible for protection under the Lanham Act necessarily includes some members that are inherently distinctive.

The Court's decision rests on the fundamental recognition that the perspective of the public is primary:

> The attribution of inherent distinctiveness to certain categories of word marks and product packaging derives from the fact that the very purpose of attaching a particular word to a product, or encasing it in a distinctive packaging, is most often to identify the source of the product. Although the words and packaging can serve subsidiary functions—a suggestive word mark (such as "Tide" for laundry detergent), for instance, may invoke positive connotations in the consumer's mind, and a garish form of packaging (such as Tide's squat, brightly decorated plastic bottles for its liquid laundry detergent) may attract an otherwise indifferent consumer's attention on a crowded store shelf—their predominant function remains source identification. Consumers are therefore predisposed to regard those symbols as indication of the producer, which is why such symbols "almost *automatically* tell a customer that they refer to a brand" and "immediately...signal a brand or a product 'source.'" And where it is not reasonable to assume consumer predisposition to take an affixed word or packaging as indication of source—where, for example, the affixed word is descriptive of the product ("Tasty" bread) or of a geographic origin ("Georgia" peaches)—inherent distinctiveness will not be found...In the case of product design, as in the case of color, we think consumer predisposition to equate the feature with the source does not exist. Consumers are aware of the reality that, almost invariably, even the most unusual of product designs—such as a cocktail shaker shaped like a penguin—is intended not to identify the source, but to render the product itself more useful or more appealing.

This language is worth quoting at length because it shows an awareness by the Supreme Court that the central focus of trademark law should be on the consumer. We are concerned with the consumer's attention in the supermarket, or the consumer's predisposition to recognize some devices as indications of source, or the consumer's contrary tendency to recognize product features as ornamental or functional rather than an indication of source.

In the Court's view, product-configuration trade dress is never a thing that intrinsically identifies source to consumers. The Court rejects the possibility that a test could be devised to determine if that were the case: "[W]here product design is concerned we have little confidence that a reasonably clear test can be devised."

Although not specifically stated, the decision conveys a sense of overall dissatisfaction with the judicial attempts to determine where trade dress in general is inherently distinctive:

> To the extent there are close cases, we believe that courts should err on the side of caution and classify ambiguous trade dress as product design, thereby requiring secondary meaning. The very closeness will suggest the existence of relatively small utility in adopting an inherent-distinctiveness principle, and relatively great consumer benefit in requiring a demonstration of secondary meaning.

The *Wal-Mart* decision leaves many issues open for debate. Is it necessarily true that product configuration can never be inherently distinctive? If there are some such configurations, should they not be entitled to protection without a showing of secondary meaning? Does not the reasoning of *Two Pesos* still require that possibility? Already there are efforts underway for legislation to overrule that aspect of the *Wal-Mart* holding. There also will be continued debate on the meaning of inherent distinctiveness for packaging trade dress, although the problems may be less difficult than with product-configuration trade dress.

While these debates will continue, the Supreme Court's decision can have a positive impact. As we think through these issues, we should focus first on the perspective of the public—what it means for a device to actually be distinctive and protectable—and then only secondarily on the categories and factors for making that determination. Further, we should not allow the tests to become ends in themselves, separated from the real issue of consumer perception.

CONCLUSION

In another context, the Supreme Court held that color was capable of protection as a trademark, stating: "It is the source-distinguishing ability of a mark—not its ontological status as a color, shape, fragrance, word, or sign—that permits it to serve these basic purposes [as a mark]."[28] The same principle should be applied in our thinking about trade dress. It is the source-indicating ability of the trade dress—not its ontological status as descriptive, suggestive, arbitrary or fanciful—that matters. We err when we depart from that understanding.

In the future, instead of debating whether a trade dress should be categorized as inherently distinctive or only protectable with secondary meaning, we might instead consider issues more central to the primary goal of trademark law. Is the public likely to be confused? This reasoning may lead us from the inquiries we have been making to slightly different questions and considerations. Does the trade dress create any impression on the public mind? How does it do that? What are the impressions created? Are those impressions protectable? If so, does the defendant's trade dress create the same or similar impressions? Is the public likely to be confused as a result?

I do not suggest that these questions are novel. Rather, it is my point that they have been present all along. To the extent, however, that such questions have been obscured behind a layer of other concerns—behind a layer of categories, factors and analytical distinctions—we may be falling short of the central goals of trademark law. Refocusing on these questions may bring us closer to those goals. Trade dress seems to be an area in particular need of this refocus as the debate over protection continues.

17

USING PATENTS AND COPYRIGHTS TO CREATE STRONG BRANDS

Trademarks, copyright and patents are typically viewed as insular rights. Too often, little thought is given to the benefits of leverage and synergy arising from a more comprehensive view and action plan. Trademark lawyers should consider the potential of other intellectual property rights to add value to a company's trademark portfolio. This article provides an introduction to the opportunities and risks involved in using patents and copyrights to create and build strong brands.

THE PATENT AND COPYRIGHT MONOPOLY

The United States Constitution provides for the exclusive protection of patents and copyrights for a limited period of time to encourage invention and creativity for the ultimate benefit of the public. Article 1, Section 8 of the U.S. Constitution states, in relevant part:

> Congress shall have the Power…To promote the Progress of Science and useful Arts, by securing for limited Times to Authors and Inventors the exclusive Right to their respective Writings and Discoveries.

Based on that Constitutional provision, Congress has enacted laws granted inventors, designers and authors the opportunity for a monopoly on the exploitation of their works in the marketplace for set periods of time.

Utility patents provide an exclusive monopoly in the sale of the patented invention for a period of twenty years.[1] Design patents provide a monopoly in a "new, original and ornamental design" for fourteen years.[2] Copyright provides a monopoly on works of authorship for a period of 95 years or more, depending on the nature of the author.[3]

PROTECTION OF TRADEMARKS AND TRADE DRESS

In contrast to patent and copyright, trademark rights are not a government created monopoly. The ability of Congress to regulate trademarks arises from the commerce clause of the U.S. Constitution, Article 1, Section 8, which provides that Congress has the power "to regulate Commerce...among the several states." Thus, trademark rights are protected by the courts to prevent deception of the public as to the source of goods in commerce. Trademark rights survive as long as the mark continues to be used and recognized as an indication of source of goods or services.

In the United States, and in some other jurisdictions, trademark rights are created by use, not registration. Marks that are coined (EXXON for petroleum products), arbitrary (APPLE for computers) or suggestive (EVERREADY for batteries) are considered inherently distinctive and can be protected upon use in commerce. Descriptive marks are not inherently distinctive and must acquire distinctiveness before they are entitled to protection. Federal law provides that five years of use is prima facie evidence of acquired distinctiveness, or secondary meaning.[4]

The overall appearance of product packaging is protectable under the trademark laws as trade dress in the same manner as words. Thus, inherently distinctive trade dress is entitled to protection upon use, but descriptive trade dress must first acquire secondary meaning before it is protected.[5] Product configuration, on the other hand, may only be protected under the trademark laws upon a showing of acquired distinctiveness.[6]

USING PATENTS TO BUILD AND CREATE A STRONG TRADEMARK

Because patents create a period of exclusive use in the marketplace, patent protection can be leveraged to establish or enhance trademark rights. A descriptive mark used in connection with the patented product may, under appropriate circumstances, enjoy a sufficient period of exclusive use sufficient to create secondary meaning. The patent monopoly also provides a period of exclusivity that can be used to increase brand awareness of marks that have inherent or acquired distinctiveness, thereby increasing the potential scope of protection available to the marks. During the period of exclusivity, the mark also has the potential to acquire fame as sufficient to obtain protection as a famous mark under the U.S. dilution laws.[7]

If the mark selected as an indication of source is not accompanied by other terms used to identify the type of product, the mark is likely to be perceived by the public as a generic term rather than an indication of source. As a result, the mark used to identify the patented product could become unenforceable as a trademark and subject to cancellation. This unhappy outcome is seen in many celebrated cases.

In *Dupont Cellophane Co. v. Waxed Products Co.*, Dupont sought to enforce rights in the mark CELLOPHANE for a patented product consisting of a transparent film.[8] The court described the origin of the mark as follows:

> The product and use of cellophane in commerce is attributed to one Brandenberger, of Bezons, France, at about the year 1909. He coined the word "cellophane" as suggesting a product made of cellulose and transparent...It would have served as a useful trade-mark, at least in the beginning, if it had not almost immediately lost ground as such because it was employed to describe the article itself. Indeed, no other descriptive word was adopted.

The mark was also used in a generic sense in the patent, which stated, "The invention relates to a label made of cellophane." The plaintiff's marketing efforts also "tended to make cellophane a generic term descriptive of the product rather than of its origin."

The Court held as a matter of law that the expiration of the relevant patents for the product "terminated any right...to the exclusive use of the name cellophane so far as it had become merely descriptive of the product itself." The fact that the plaintiff had registered the term as a trademark gave it no right to monopolize use of the term in its descriptive, generic sense. As a result, the defendant, and others, had the right use the name "cellophane" to identify the product they were allowed to sell as long as they did not mislead customers into believing that the product came from the DuPont. There was no violation of rights as long as the source of the cellophane was identified.

The *DuPont* case shows that even a coined mark can be lost if the manufacturer allows the mark to be used to identify or describe the product itself, rather than as an indication of source.

A similar result was obtained before the Supreme Court in *Kellogg Co. v. National Biscuit Co.*[9] Nabisco had enjoyed a patent monopoly in the manufacture of pillow-shaped shredded wheat biscuits sold under the name SHREDDED WHEAT. When the patent for making the product expired, Kellogg entered the market using the name "Shredded Wheat" for a similar product. The Court rejected Nabisco's objection because the term "shredded wheat" identified the article, not the source of the article:

> The plaintiff has no exclusive right to the use of the term "Shredded Wheat" as a trade name. For that is the generic term of the article, which describes it with a fair degree of accuracy; and is the term by which the biscuit in pillow-shaped form is generally known by the public...As Kellogg Company had the right to make the article, it had, also, the right to use the term by which the public knows it.

The Court explained that effect of the expiration of the patent on rights in the term used for the patent product:

> The basic patent for the product and for the process of making it...issued...In those patents the term "shredded" is repeatedly used as descriptive of the product...Since during the life of the patents "Shredded Wheat" was the general designation of the patented product, there passed to the public upon the expiration of the patent, not only the right to make the article as it was made during the patent period, but also the right to apply thereto the name by which it had become known...

The Court further held that the SHREDDED WHEAT was not entitled to protection even if Nabisco could show secondary meaning or acquired distinctiveness. It had become a generic term which could be used by all. As a result, Kellogg, and others, were free to use the name SHREDDED WHEAT for the product, as long as they identified the source of the goods in a non-confusing manner.

AVOIDING GENERIC USE— THE NUTRASWEET BRAND

NUTRASWEET is a well-known example of the use of the patent monopoly to create a brand without allowing the mark to become generic. The product itself is a sweetener discovered at G.D. Searle and Company by James Schlatter in 1965.

The term "aspartame" was coined as the generic description of the product. NUTRASWEET became the trademark for the sweetener in 1980. By combining the trademark NUTRASWEET with an easily remembered generic term (as opposed to a complicated name for a chemical compound) Searle avoided the risk that the public would use NUTRASWEET as the generic term for the new product. Searle was also able to use the period of patent exclusivity to obtain market share and brand awareness for NUTRASWEET brand aspartame sweetener. Upon the expiration of the patents, others are permitted to sell the same sweetener and use the generic name "aspartame", but Searle and its successor have been able to maintain NUTRASWEET as a strong brand.

It is easy to imagine the NUTRASWEET brand suffering the same fate as "cellophane" if Searle had not also created the term aspartame to identify the patented product.

STRATEGIES FOR BRAND BUILDING

The three situations described above suggest several strategic considerations for leveraging patent rights to create and build a strong brand.

1. Careful planning and marketing strategies are needed to avoid the loss of the brand as a generic term.

2. Trademark counsel should ensure that the brand is not used generically in the patent submissions.

3. Secondary terms should be selected or developed as generic or descriptive terms for the patented product.

4. Technical documents, as well as advertising, should be reviewed to avoid generic use.

5. Marketing strategies should be employed to increase market share and brand awareness during the patent monopoly to create brand loyalty so that customers will prefer the company's branded product after the expiration of the patent.

6. Special forms of advertising may be needed to create recognition of the brand as a trademark and not a generic term.

7. Selection of a coined or arbitrary mark facilitates the development of a strong brand.

CREATING TRADE DRESS PROTECTION FOR PRODUCT CONFIGURATION

The patent monopoly can also be useful to help establish trade dress rights in product features and configuration. Under U.S. law, product configuration can be protected under trademark laws if it is distinctive and nonfunctional. The Supreme Court ruled in *Wal-Mart Stores, Inc. v. Samara Brothers, Inc.*, however, that product design is never deemed inherently distinctive and therefore may only be protected under the trademark laws upon a showing that it has acquired distinctiveness, or secondary meaning, as an indication of source.[10]

The monopoly provided by utility or design patents affords a period of market exclusivity that may be sufficient to establish secondary meaning as a result of use and advertising. It is likely, however, that mere sales may not be sufficient unless supported by advertising and promotion that features the product design as an indication of source.

THE FUNCTIONALITY RISK

In addition to showing secondary meaning, it is also necessary under U.S. law to show that the product design in which trademark rights are claimed is nonfunctional. The Supreme Court has explained that trade dress protection may not be claimed for any product feature that is functional.[11] Federal law establishes that the burden of proving nonfunctionality belongs to the party claiming rights in trade dress that is not registered as a trademark.[12]

The mere fact that a claimed feature has a useful function does not necessarily mean it is legally functional and ineligible for protection under the trademark laws. Instead, a feature is deemed legally functional "if it is essential to the use or purpose of the article or if it affects the cost or quality of the article,"[13] or if exclusive use of it "would put competitors at a significant non-reputation-related disadvantage,"[14] Otherwise, the feature may be entitled to trade dress protection even if it has a useful function.

A expired patent may have an adverse effect on a claim for trade dress protection because it is evidence that the claimed feature is functional. As stated by the Supreme Court in the *Traffix* case:

> A utility patent is strong evidence that the features therein claimed are functional. If trade dress protection is sought for those features the strong evidence of functionality based on the previous patent adds great weight to the statu-

tory presumption that the features are deemed functional until proved otherwise by the party seeking trade dress protection. Where the expired patent claimed the features in question, one who seeks to establish trade dress protection must carry the heavy burden of showing that the feature is not functional, for instance by showing that the it is merely an ornamental, incidental, or arbitrary aspect of the device.

In *Traffix*, the Court concluded that the claimed feature—a dual-spring design for a flexible road sign—was functional based on the evidentiary inference of functionality arising from disclosure of the design in an expired utility patent. The Court went on to note that features disclosed in a patent might still be entitled to trade dress protection in other circumstances:

> In a case where a manufacturer seeks to protect arbitrary, incidental, or ornamental aspects of features of a product found in the patent claims, such as arbitrary curves in the legs or an ornamental pattern painted on the springs, a different result might obtain. There the manufacturer could perhaps prove that those aspects do not serve a purpose within the terms of the utility patent.

The Court also explained the rationale for denying trade dress protection to functional design:

> The Lanham Act does not exist to reward manufacturers for their innovation in creating a particular device; that is the purpose of patent law and its period of exclusivity. The Lanham Act, furthermore, does not protect trade dress in a functional design simply because an investment has been made to encourage the public to associate a particular functional feature with a single manufacturer or seller.

The *Traffix* decision demonstrates the difficulty in claiming trade dress rights in product design disclosed in an expired utility patent. The mere fact that the object is useful increases the chance that it may be deemed functional. Further, the expired utility patent will be considered "strong evidence of functionality." Obviously this is a difficult standard to meet, but it may still be possible to demonstrate trade dress rights in a feature disclosed in a utility patent. For example, in *Clamp Mfg. Co. v. Enco Mfg. Co.*,[15] the court held the particular design of a formerly patented C-clamp was nonfunctional because competitors could compete effectively without copying the design and several other designs were available.

Although the *Enco* case pre-dates *Traffix*, it illustrates a strategy for overcoming the adverse evidentiary presumption flowing from the patent. *Traffix* indicates that lack of competitive necessity is not sufficient to avoid a find of functionality if the design is essential to the use or purpose of the device or if it affects the cost or quality of the device. Nevertheless, proof that the particular design is not essential to the purpose of the device could include the same kind of showing that was successful in *Enco*.

Some courts and commentators have argued that features disclosed in a patent should not be protectable as trade dress even if nonfunctional and distinctive. As explained in *Vornado Air Circulation System Inc. v. Duracraft Corp.*,[16] trade dress protection should be denied because protecting a "significant inventive aspect" of the patented invention under trademark laws would interfere with the core patent goal of permitting competitors from copying from expired utility patents and would conflict with the Constitutional purpose of patent protection. Proponents of this position argue that the inventor of the device makes a bargain with the government: when she elects to have a period of patent exclusivity, she agrees in exchange that the device will fall into the public domain upon the expiration of the patent. It is a breach of that bargain to use the trademark laws in an attempt to extend that exclusivity beyond the term of the patent. The Court in *Traffix* acknowledged but did not resolve this question, stating there will be time enough to consider the matter if the proper case arises.

Although design patents also afford a limited period of exclusivity, they do not entail the same evidentiary presumption of functionality as a utility patent, since design patent protection may only be claimed in features that are ornamental. Thus, a number of courts have granted trade dress protection to product configuration covered by a design patent.[17]

COPYRIGHT AS SURROGATE FOR TRADEMARK RIGHTS

Although copyrightable subject matter does not include words and short phrases, many of the devices typically protected under trademark laws—logos, label designs, packaging, product designs—may be protected as copyrightable subject matter. In some cases, such protection may have several advantages over trademark protection. Under U.S. law, copyright protection is available immediately upon creation. It does not require use in commerce or distinctiveness. The use of a copyright notice is no longer a requirement for protection. To establish copyright infringement, it is not necessary to show a likelihood of confusion. Rather, proof of access and substantial similarity is sufficient. The copyright statute also provides the possibility of obtaining statutory damages in lieu of actual damages, and attorneys fees are available to the prevailing party.

Although copyright protection is not limited by the requirement of functionality, protection is not available for "useful articles" unless the work includes artistic elements that are physically or conceptually separable from the work.[18]

An example often cited of a device eligible for protection under both copyright and trademark law is the shape of a Mickey Mouse telephone. Although the device is a useful article, the Mickey Mouse form is independent of the article's function. Accordingly, it could be protected under copyright law. In addition, the Mickey Mouse design also serves as an indication of source specific to Disney and is protectable as a trademark.[19]

Imagine the introduction of an analogous product design under current law. Following the rule in *Traffix*, it is likely that the product design could not be protected as a trademark until it had enjoyed use sufficient to establish secondary meaning. Under copyright law, however, the design would be eligible for protection immediately upon creation. Thus, copyright protection could be used to prevent infringement before trademark protection is available and could be used to supplement trademark protection after secondary meaning is established.

CONCLUSION

Various strategies are available for using patents and copyrights as an enhancement to or substitute for trademark protection. The exclusive monopoly afforded under patent law provides an opportunity to build secondary meaning or brand awareness until the brand emerges strong and able to overcome infringements without reliance on the patent. Copyright may be used as a supplement or substitute for protection of some logos and trade dress, offering the possibility of immediate protection, simplified issues of proof and enhanced damages. The strategies are accompanied by risks and limits. By understanding the basic issues, trademark attorneys can help clients and their companies create and build stronger trademark rights.

18

TRADEMARK LICENSING IN A CORPORATE TRANSACTION

Trademark rights pose special problems in a corporate transaction. Because trademark rights involves legal issues that are not attendant to other forms of property, intellectual or real, unique problems can arise. Two key areas of concern are the requirement of quality control and the potential for the loss of rights if the transaction results in the splitting of trademark rights.

THE QUALITY CONTROL REQUIREMENT

Licensing and Identification of Source

By definition, a trademark is any device that serves as an indication of source. When a trademark is licensed, how does it continue to serve as an indication of source? It does so, the theory goes, if the licensor controls the nature and quality of the goods. Then, the licensee is merely an arm of the licensor and the source-indicating function of the trademark is preserved. Licensing without such control is called licensing in gross or naked licensing, and may cause the mark to lose its source-indicating function. In such circumstances, enforceable rights in the trademark may be lost. This basic principle is often overlooked by the business person or counsel, who are inclined to treat trademarks as ordinary property rights such as patents, which they are not.

Historical Roots

Originally at common law, the licensing of a trademark resulted in an abandonment of rights because the mark was no longer associated with a single source.[1]

Over time, however, the common law caught up with the commercial realities of the marketplace, and licensing of trademarks was allowed if the licensor controlled the nature and quality of the goods or services involved.[2] This principle continues to be stretched to the limit by the demands of the market, raising the question of how the manufacturer of motorcycles can exercise meaningful control over the nature and quality of HARLEY-DAVIDSON cigarettes, the maker of soft drinks over COCA-COLA clothing, and the producer of a movie over STAR WARS toys, trading cards and cereal. Indeed, how can the Chicago Cubs, who can't control a baseball game, control the nature and quality of hats, T-shirts and jackets? The answer lies in the definition of a trademark as a source-indicating device. As long as the licensee acts as an arm of the licensor the goods continue to have a single source.

Abandonment Based on Lack of Quality Control

Does a lack of quality control necessarily result in an abandonment of rights or is it merely evidence of abandonment? While the black letter principle is well-established, it is rarely enforced to produce the draconian consequence of a total loss of rights in a mark. The courts seek to avoid a forfeiture of rights when a defendant raises the issue to defend a claim of infringement, and the issue rarely arises in other circumstances. Typically, in such cases, the courts will accept the slimmest evidence of quality control as sufficient.[3] Although many question its continuing merit in our modern marketing world, the quality control requirement continues to have force: the failure to exercise meaningful quality control over licensees can still result in the loss of trademark rights.[4]

STATUTORY BASIS FOR THE REQUIREMENT

Although the requirement of quality control is black letter trademark law, what is the statutory authority for the requirement? Why does a lack of quality control result in a loss of trademark rights? The Lanham Act contains no specific provision that requires quality control as a condition of valid licensing. Instead, the requirement is the result of a combination of provisions.

15 U.S.C. §1127 defines a trademark as any "device" used "to identify and distinguish his or her goods, including a unique product, from those manufactured or sold by others and to indicate the source of the goods…"

15 U.S.C. §1127 also states that rights in a mark may be deemed abandoned, and therefore unenforceable, "when any course of conduct of the owner, includ-

ing acts of omission as well as commission, causes the mark...to lose its signifi-cance as a mark..." Thus, if a mark is no longer used to indicate a particular source, the result may be an abandonment of rights. How does licensing avoid this risk?

15 U.S.C. §1055 provides that use by a related company "shall inure to the benefit of the registrant [or owner of the mark] and "shall not affect the validity of such mark or registration, provided such mark is not used in such a manner as to deceive the public."

15 U.S.C. 1127§ defines a related company as any person who "is controlled by the registrant...in respect to the nature and quality of the goods or services in connection with which the mark is used."

These provisions lead us to question whether a lack of quality control neces-sarily results in abandonment or whether we must still determine if the mark has in fact lost its significance as an indication of source? I favor the latter view, but court *dicta* often suggests that the lack of quality control alone is sufficient. The latter view is also supported by recent decisions where the lack of quality control did not result in a loss of rights because, for example, "the particular circum-stances of the licensing arrangement indicate the public will not be deceived."[5]

WHAT IS ADEQUATE QUALITY CONTROL?

The level of control required to meet the quality control requirement in trade-mark licensing has progressively declined, to the point where many courts have accepted only minimal controls as sufficient. It remains clear, however, that the exercise of quality control, not merely the right to exercise quality control, is important. The licensor may conduct its own inspections or delegate the author-ity to a third party. Where there is a sufficiently close relationship between the licensor and licensee (same officers, family relationship, etc.) sufficient quality control may result from the relationship alone. In a limited number of cases, quality control by the licensee has been deemed sufficient, but this is a dangerous approach for the licensor since it puts the continued validity of the mark out of the licensor's control.

THE ADVERSE EFFECTS OF QUALITY CONTROL

Can too much quality control be a bad thing? Strong control may also increase a licensor's liability for the acts of a licensee.[6]

THE RISK OF MISHANDLED ASSIGNMENTS

In corporate transactions, the risks of mishandling trademarks are high. The consequences range from weakened rights to total abandonment of valuable trademarks with long term licensing and litigation problems in between. These problems can arise when the transaction involves part of a business operated under a house mark. Assuming, for example, that the goal of the transaction is to sell certain subsidiaries as they are currently operated while continuing in business with the other subsidiaries, what happens to the house mark? Several principles apply.

LOSS OF RIGHTS

First, a transaction which results in the ownership of the same mark by unrelated companies for similar goods may destroy the mark. As defined in 15 U.S.C. §1127, a mark may be deemed abandoned when any acts or omissions of the other cause the mark to lose its significance as a mark, that is, lose the ability to distinguish one company's goods or services from another. If two unrelated companies both use the same name for similar goods, the name may cease to function as a trademark for either.

A good example of this problem is *Heaton Enterprises of Nevada v. Lang.*[7] Heaton, the original trademark owner, started a pizza parlor in Iowa under the name MINSKY'S. It sold the pizza parlor with the right to use the name, but reserved the right to use the name itself in another business. It opened up another pizza parlor, also called MINSKY'S, then sold that one with the right to use the name. This process continued. In the end there were many unrelated owners using the MINSKY name for pizza parlors. Lang, a trustee of the Minsky estate, also sought to use the MINSKY'S name, for pizza parlors, and Heaton opposed. The Trademark Trial and Appeal Board ruled against Heaton. By selling the businesses and allowing unrelated companies to be using the same name, the Heaton had lost all rights in the mark.

DISTINCT AND SEPARABLE BUSINESSES

The second principle is a corollary of the first. In general, rights in a mark may be split between "distinct and separable" businesses. As always, the test should focus on the public perception, whether or not the relevant public would likely assume that the goods coming from the assigned portion were controlled by the retained business or not.

For example, in *Gentry Canning Company v. Blue Ribbon Growers, Inc.*[8] the Oakford Company had assigned its rights in the BLUE RIBBON trademark for tea to a company that was not involved in the later litigation. Later, Oakford assigned its rights in the BLUE RIBBON mark for canned fruits and vegetables to the predecessor of Blue Ribbon Growers, Inc., one of the parties in the litigation. Then Gentry Canning Company used BLUE RIBBON for canned vegetables, sought registration and was denied. It petitioned to cancel Blue Ribbon Growers' registration on the grounds that the BLUE RIBBON mark for tea on one hand, and canned fruits and vegetables on the other, resulted in an abandonment of the mark.

The Board dismissed the petition, stating: "[w]hat we have here is a party who owned a number of registrations covering the mark BLUE RIBBON and design for a large number of grocery products, and assigned one registration for one distinct phase of its business to one party, and a number of registrations concerned with another distinct phase of its operations, particularly of interest to a canner or a packer, to another party." Thus, rights in a mark may be split when different but arguably related products are involved.

These cases illustrate two very different results: splitting ownership of a mark between identical pizza parlor services results in abandonment, but splitting ownership between tea and canned vegetables does not. How close can the line be drawn? The following cases are instructive.

In *Gould Engineering Co. v. Goebel*,[9] the GOULD name was split between oil and oil burners. The issue was whether that split resulted in an abandonment of the mark. The court held that it had not.

In *Texaco, Inc. v. Kane County Oil, Inc.*,[10] Texaco purchased an oil business called McCormack OIL. McCormack reserved the right to use the McCormack name on its tire dealership. Later, there was a dispute as to whether splitting the McCormack mark between the oil company and the tire dealership had resulted in an abandonment. The court held that there was no abandonment because the McCormack oil business and the McCormack tire dealership were distinct and separable businesses.

WEAKENED RIGHTS

The third principle qualifies the second. Even if the assignment is valid, splitting ownership rights in a mark between unrelated parties may weaken the value and enforceability of the mark.

The classic case in this area is *California Fruit Growers Exchange v. Sunkist Baking Co.*[11] The California Fruit Growers Exchange used the mark SUNKIST for fruit and soft drinks. The California Packing Corporation, an unrelated entity, used SUNKIST for canned and dried fruits and vegetables. By contract, the two agreed to co-exist.

Together they sued Sunkist Baking Company for using SUNKIST on bread. The Court of Appeals held that if the Exchange and the Baking Company could agree to co-exist without confusion, then they could not be heard to complain about the use of the same mark for bread.

Similarly, in *Campbell Soup Co. v. Armour & Co.*[12] Carnation, which had a white and red label for milk, and Campbell, which had a red and white label for soup, agreed to coexist in their respective product lines. Carnation and Campbell sued Armour for using a red and white label. The district court focused on the agreement to co-exist, stating: "The essence of a trademark is that it shall be a true badge of origin in indicating that the contents to which it is affixed is the product of the trademark proprietor and no others…It is vital to the existence of a trademark that it should be used by one and by only one concern. A trademark cannot serve two masters; it cannot identify two sources at the same time and remain a trademark."

STRATEGIC OPTIONS

For these reasons, there are clear risks in a transaction that splits ownership of a mark. Fortunately, there are other options.

One possibility is to use a concurrent use agreement. The Federal Circuit in several cases has said that the opinion of businessmen on an issue of confusion as reflected in such agreements should be given great weight. Thus, a concurrent use agreement might avoid the problem of splitting rights in a mark. Unfortunately, concurrent use agreements are not always accepted. They may not be given weight if they constitute a naked consent or if a finding of likelihood of confusion is unavoidable. They also do not avoid a weakening of rights under the Sunkist Doctrine.

Licenses are another way to address this problem. With proper control, the use by the licensee will inure to the benefit of the licensor. Thus, licenses, can avoid the problems that arise from splitting marks. Licenses pose other issues however. For example, there is the risk to the licensee that the license may be lost if the licensor goes bankrupt.

Another approach is joint ownership as shown in *In re Diamond Walnut Growers Inc.*[13] That case allowed two parties to claim joint ownership of a mark that was then used by a joint venture.

Finally, the issues has sometimes been addressed by assigning the mark to a holding company which then licenses the mark to the respective businesses. For example, in *The Ritz Hotel v. Charles of the Ritz*[14] separate parties claimed rights in the RITZ mark. The problem was resolved by placing the mark in a holding company co-owned by both parties.

The proper handling of trademarks in corporate transactions is an important and difficult issue. Trademark counsel should be involved in the entire process to insure that valuable rights are preserved.

19

KEY LICENSING CONSIDERATIONS

There are various circumstances in which trademarks can be licensed. Each presents particular considerations that may differ from transaction to transaction. However, common concerns arise in most trademark licensing situations. The essential provisions of a trademark license agreements and the key interests of the licensor are outlined below.

USE OF TRADEMARKS

A trademark owner controls the manner in which its trademarks are used to insure a consistent marketing identity and to maintain the validity of the marks. To maximize its protection, the licensor should clearly set forth guidelines regulating uses of its trademarks.

The Licensor's Goals:

- Set forth the manner in which others may use the licensor's trademarks in as detailed a manner as possible.

- Prevent use of the licensor trademarks as part of the other party's trademark, domain name or trade name.

- Prohibit any sale, transfer, assignment, or sub-license of trademark rights.

RIGHTS IN TRADEMARKS

A trademark owner wants to protect its ownership rights in the marks and avoid conflicts over the validity of its marks. Without provisions acknowledging the trademark owner's rights, the other party may have more latitude to challenge the ownership or validity of the trademarks.

The Licensor's Goals:

- Require the other party to recognize the licensor's ownership of the marks and the validity of and the licensor trademark registrations.

- Obtain an agreement not to dispute the licensor's ownership of the marks or their validity.

- Prevent the other party from applying for registration of the licensor's marks.

- Receive commitment to cooperate with the licensor in maintaining the licensor's ownership of the marks.

QUALITY CONTROL/QUALITY ASSURANCE

Trademark licensors have an affirmative duty to ensure the licensee's use of the trademarks comply with the licensor's quality standards. Lack of quality control can result in the licensor's loss of rights in its trademarks. Agreement alone is probably not sufficient to satisfy the obligations of a licensor of trademarks. An ongoing program of actual quality control is necessary. Therefore, it is essential that the licensor set forth quality standards in the license agreements and then follow through by actively enforcing those standards.

The Licensor's Goals:

- Insure that licensed products meet approved specifications.

- Insure that advertising by licensees and others is consistent with our image and specifications.

- Inspect samples of the licensee's products prior to their being used.

- Maintain the right to inspect products, packaging, advertising and other marketing materials.

- Require the other party to comply with the licensor's determination of a deficiency.

ENFORCEMENT

A trademark owner must police and maintain its trademarks to prevent third parties from using the marks and weakening the owner's rights. When the licensor is granting nonexclusive permission or licenses, the enforcement provisions should require the other party to inform the licensor of any infringing activities, and allow the licensor, rather than the other party, to take action against infringers.

The Licensor's Goals:

- Require the other party to promptly inform the licensor of any unauthorized or infringing uses of the licensor's trademarks.

- Reserve the right to take action against any infringing or unauthorized users.

- Require the other party to cooperate and provide evidence in actions against infringing or unauthorized users.

INDEMNIFICATION

A trademark owner often includes an indemnification clause in trademark agreements to protect itself from claims that may arise from use authorized under the agreement. The indemnification typically will not include third party claims that the licensor's trademarks themselves infringe the rights of that third party. The licensor should include such a provision in its trademark agreements to insulate itself from liability that relates to the grantee's advertising, marketing, or promotion using the licensor's trademarks or the manufacture, sale or use of licensed products.

The Licensor's Goals:

- Require prompt notice of any claims relating to the licensor's trademarks.

- Ensure the other party indemnifies the licensor against claims arising from or relating to the licensee's activities.

DURATION

The agreement should specify a term to ensure that it is not interpreted as a permanent assignment of rights. The licensor should clearly set forth the end date of each agreement, while including a clause that enables the parties to extend the agreement if they so desire.

TERMINATION

The agreement should include a termination provision to set forth the conditions under which the agreement will end, as well as the parties' obligations following the termination. To maintain its rights to terminate, the licensor must specify the particular reasons when it may terminate the agreement, as well as the post-termination process. Although unenforceable by current federal statute, provisions calling for termination in the event of bankruptcy are included to reflect the intent of the parties and the possibility of changes in the bankruptcy laws.

The Licensor's Goals:

- Ensure it has an unconditional right to terminate the agreements, subject to a notice provision.

- Reserve the right to terminate for any breach, particularly regarding the use and quality of the licensor's trademarks.

- Maintain the right to terminate if the other party seeks legal relief for financial difficulties to prevent creditors or any other third parties from claiming rights to the agreement.

- Require the other party to immediately cease using the licensor's trademarks upon termination of the agreements.

20

VALIDITY OF REGISTRATION NOT REVIVED AFTER ABANDONMENT

Companies occasionally discontinue use of registered marks and resume use later. They should realize the legal dangers inherent in this pattern. The United States Trademark Trial and Appeal Board has granted summary judgment confirming that the validity of trademark registration cannot be revived after abandonment by resumption of use of the mark or intent to resume its use. This decision offers important insight for U.S. trademark holders seeking to avoid the loss of rights.[1]

Trademark nonuse is a greater threat to trademark rights under U.S. law than under the law of many foreign countries where nonuse is curable. For example, in the British law countries, Argentina and France, the courts have concluded that resumption of trademark use before the commencement of a cancellation action will cure nonuse and avoid cancellation. Similarly, the European Community Directive to approximate national trademark laws and the draft Community Trademark Regulation provide, with certain qualifications, that resumption of use cures prior nonuse. In contrast, in the U.S. and in over thirty other jurisdictions, as a general rule, nonuse for the statutory period is not curable and will result in loss of trademark rights.

Nabisco Brands Inc. (Nabisco) filed a petition to cancel a registration for the mark SUPREME for "biscuits, cakes, crackers, cookies, wafers," owned by the Keebler Company (Keebler). Nabisco claimed that Keebler had not used the mark since at least 1970 and had no intent to resume use of the mark between at least 1970 and 1983. Keebler argued that its good faith intent to resume use of the SUPREME was demonstrated by market testing of the mark on numerous product lines after 1983. Keebler also claimed that the issue of abandonment had already been decided in Keebler's favor in a prior preliminary injunction action between the parties and that the district court's preliminary injunction ruling had preclusive effect in the cancellation proceeding.

CLAIM PRECLUSION

The Board ruled that Nabisco's claims were not precluded by the prior civil action for two reasons. First, the Board noted that a court's determination on a preliminary injunction generally will not have preclusive effect on a subsequent proceeding because the ruling is interlocutory and does not constitute a final determination on the merits of the case. Second, the Board recognized that preclusion does not apply where the parties voluntarily stipulate to dismiss an action without prejudice. In the instant case, the written agreement between the parties that resulted in the voluntary dismissal specifically stated that "Nabisco shall have the right to pursue Cancellation No. 21,498 with respect to Keebler's Registration No. 124,976 for the mark before the Trademark Trial and Appeal Board or by appeal of its decision to the United States Court of Appeals for the Federal Circuit."

ABANDONMENT

Under U.S. trademark law at the time of the proceeding, a mark is deemed abandoned when "its use has been discontinued with intent not to resume such use. Nonuse for three consecutive years shall be prima facie abandonment."[2]

Nabisco established that Keebler had made no use of the SUPREME mark in connection with the goods identified in the disputed registration during at least the period from 1970 to 1979. Keebler did not disprove the underlying fact of nonuse and failed to introduce any evidence, such as development plans, market tests or advertisements, to demonstrate an intent to resume use of the mark during the period from 1970 through 1979. Its evidence of marketing plans and tests involving the SUPREME mark after 1979 was unavailing. The Board held that later efforts cannot cure a prior abandonment. Even subsequent re adoption of the involved mark would represent a new and separate use, but would not prevent cancellation of the registration. Accordingly, Nabisco's motion for summary judgment was granted on the claim of abandonment.

COMMENT

Under U.S. trademark law, nonuse alone is not sufficient to establish abandonment. There must also be an "intent not to resume use." That intent may be presumed when there has been three years of nonuse. To prevent abandonment in the face of three years of nonuse, the registrant must come forward with evidence of an intent to resume use sufficient to rebut the presumption of an intent not to resume use. Although such evidence may include marketing plans, market tests, or similar activities that do not constitute actual use, the evidence must be relevant to the period of nonuse. It is not sufficient to show such efforts after the mark has been abandoned.

Attorneys responsible for trademark maintenance should evaluate their clients' portfolios to determine if any marks may have been abandoned due to nonuse. If so, counsel should advise management that the unused marks are at risk and attempt to document any marketing efforts during the period of nonuse that may demonstrate an intent to resume use.

21

TRADEMARK PARODY AND THE FIRST AMENDMENT: HUMOR IN THE EYE OF THE BEHOLDER

Trademark parody has become increasingly common in the United States. The use of another's trademark in a humorous or disparaging manner can appear in many forms, from gag products,[1] to slogans and advertising for an unrelated product,[2] to satiric commentary.[3] While "[i]n one sense a parody is an attempt to derive benefit from the reputation of the owner of the mark...a parody relies upon a difference from the original mark, presumably a humorous difference, in order to produce its desired effect."[4] A parody must convey two simultaneous and contradictory messages. It must express that it is the original, while at the same time, that it is not the original but instead is a parody. As one court stated, "[t]o the extent it does only the former [that it is the original] but not the latter [that it is not the original], it is not only a poor parody but also vulnerable under the trademark law."

The first Amendment to the United States Constitution guarantees free speech and artistic expression.[5] Since parodies involve a form of expression, they are entitled to protection against undue government interference.[6] Traditionally, the First Amendment interests have been adequately protected by the standard likelihood of confusion analysis. The defendant's First Amendment interests end when the parody creates a likelihood of confusion.[7] However, more recently there has been a trend to view the First Amendment issue separately, particularly when the parody involves a commentary, as opposed to a mere gag or a play on words. The First Amendment analysis attempts to balance the public interest in free speech against the public interest in avoiding confusion in the marketplace.[8] This

Article will illustrate a framework for the analysis of First Amendment protection in the context of trademark parody.

Many courts deciding trademark parody cases up until the late 1980s either dismissed the free speech issue or decided the case without reference to the free speech argument. Those courts that rejected the First Amendment argument applied the reasoning handed down by the United States Supreme Court in *Lloyd's Corp. v. Tanner.*[9] One such case was *Dallas Cowboys Cheerleaders v. Pussycat Cinema.*[10] The issue in *Tanner* was whether a privately owned shopping center could prohibit the distribution of handbills on the property when the handbilling was unrelated to the shopping center's operation. The Court held that the petitioner's privately owned shopping center was not dedicated to public use, and as such, there was no First Amendment right to distribute handbills on the property. The focus of the Court's reasoning centered on the existence of "adequate alternative avenues of communication." Where such "avenues" existed, property owners did not have to yield to others' exercise of their First Amendment rights.

In *Dallas Cowboys,* the Second Circuit addressed the question of whether the defendant filmmaker's use of the plaintiff's trademark was protected under the First Amendment. After finding that the defendant's film, which depicted women wearing uniforms similar to the plaintiff's, created a "likelihood of confusion,"[11] the court rejected the defendant's First Amendment defense. In making this determination, the court reasoned that simply because "defendant's movie may convey a barely discernible message does not entitle them to appropriate plaintiff's trademark in the process of conveying that message, and as such it need not 'yield to the exercise of the First Amendment rights under circumstances where adequate alternatives of communication exists.'" As a result, the Second Circuit Court of Appeals ruled that the district court did not encroach upon the defendant's First Amendment rights when it granted the plaintiff's preliminary injunction.

Another case that had a similar result is *Mutual of Omaha Insurance v. Novak.*[12] The *Mutual of Omaha* case involved a t-shirt that said "Mutant of Omaha," with an emaciated Indian Head on the t-shirt. The defendant claimed he was selling the t-shirts in part to express his concern over nuclear proliferation: thus, he argued, the t-shirt should be considered protected speech under the First Amendment. In rejecting the defendant's First Amendment claim, the court relied on the fact that the defendant sold t-shirts and started up a company called the Mutant of Omaha, Inc. The court held that the plaintiff's trademark was a form of property and the First Amendment did not give the defendant the right to infringe on those rights. According to the court, the property interest in a trademark "need not 'yield to the exercise of First Amendment rights under circumstances where adequate alternative avenues of communication exist.'" Accordingly, under the traditional approach, as illustrated by *Dallas Cowboys* and *Mutual of Omaha*, courts refused to balance a plaintiff's property interest in a trademark against a defendant's First Amendment interest in free expression when there were alternative means available to the defendant to convey his or her message. Once a court determined that there was a likelihood of confusion, that was the end of the inquiry and no further First Amendment analysis was undertaken.

Both the *Dallas Cowboys* court and the *Mutual of Omaha* court relied on the reasoning of the United States Supreme Court in *Tanner*. However, the applicability of *Tanner* to trademark parody remains unsettled. The situation contemplated in the *Tanner* case was very different. *Tanner* did not affect the content of the speech. Rather, it only affected the time, place or manner of delivery of the speech. The *Dallas Cowboys* case and the *Mutual of Omaha* case, however, do affect the content of speech. Therefore, the *Tanner* case does not apply in the trademark parody context. Courts and commentators began to recognize this fact in the late 1980s.

THE EVOLVING FIRST AMENDMENT ANALYSIS

The evolving standard in trademark parody cases distinguishes the nature of the communication based upon whether it is commercial or non-commercial speech. The first line of distinction in a trademark parody analysis is whether a particular advertisement or product involves artistic expression or commercial speech. If a court finds that a parody constitutes artistic expression, the First Amendment interests are balanced against the interests of the Lanham Act. For commercial speech to come within the protection afforded by the First Amendment, it must involve lawful activity and not be misleading.[13] Thus, if a court finds that a trademark parody involves commercial speech, it does not perform a balancing test. In such cases, the parody defense becomes just one factor to consider in the confusion analysis. However, distinguishing between what is commercial and what is non-commercial can be a troublesome task. In *Virginia Pharmacy Board v. Virginia Citizens Consumer Counsel*,[14] the United States Supreme Court characterized commercial speech as that which "does no more than propose a commercial transaction." That can be a difficult standard to apply in the trademark context. Often, a parody may mix commercial and non-commercial elements.

One of the first major decisions to recognize the distinction between commercial and non-commercial speech in the trademark parody context was *L. L. Bean v. Drake Publishers, Inc.*[15] The parody at issue involved a two page article entitled "L.L. Beam's Back-To-School-Sex-Catalog" placed in a monthly periodical featuring erotic entertainment. The court noted that the pervasive influence of trademarks in our society today have made recognizable trademarks a natural target for satirists.

On appeal, the court found that the parody constituted an editorial or artistic, rather than commercial, use of the plaintiff's trademark. Thus, the court considered the parody non-commercial speech. Accordingly, the court reasoned that it was unconstitutional to prevent the use of another's trademark based on dilution law when the parody was purely non-commercial, although in the context of commercial speech, anti-dilution statutes may constitute legitimate regulations of speech.

In contrast to the purely non-commercial speech found in *L. L. Bean*, in *Schiffelin & Co. v. Jack Company of Boca, Inc.*,[16] the New York District Court faced a parody involving purely commercial speech. The popcorn sold by the defendants, called Champop, was packaged in a champagne bottle similar to the Dom Perignon bottle produced by the plaintiffs. In addition, the label affixed was of identical shape and color as the Dom Perignon label. The defendants claimed that their ten-dollar bottle of popcorn would not likely be confused with Dom Perignon Champagne and that this was simply a "classic parody" protected under the First Amendment. First, the defendant was selling a product; second, the defendant did not base the parody upon artistic or political expression; and third, the underlying purpose of the parody was economic gain. Thus, the court did not balance the First Amendment rights to freedom of speech against established trademark rights. The court found that the parody was not sufficiently strong to destroy the potential for consumer confusion between the two products.[17]

In another case where the speech was purely commercial, *Carson v. Here's Johnny Portable Toilets*,[18] the Sixth Circuit held that the defendant violated Carson's right of publicity because the defendant "intentionally appropriated his identity for commercial exploitation" by using the now famous "Here's Johnny" phrase to promote their product. The defendant claimed that because neither the celebrity's name nor likeness was used, there could be no finding of infringement. The court, however, concluded that protecting the "Here's Johnny" phrase did not implicate the commands of the First Amendment.[19]

The expressive elements of parody and artistic expression require greater First Amendment protection than pure commercial speech. In *Cliffs Notes v. Bantam*

DoubleDay Dell Publishing Group,[20] the publisher of a study guide claimed that the cover of a parody publication would give consumers the false impression as to which company published the book. There, the court used a balancing test in the context of artistic speech, rather than classifying the publication as commercial speech. In balancing the interest, the court noted that:

> in deciding the reach of the Lanham Act in any case where an expressive work is alleged to infringe a trademark, it is appropriate to weigh the public interest in free expression against the public interest in avoiding consumer confusion…the expressive element of parodies requires more protection than the labeling of ordinary commercial products.

Though the court noted that there is a strong public interest in avoiding confusion, in the context of artistic expression, somewhat more risk of confusion should be tolerated. Thus, the court found that the parody embodied only a slight risk of confusion and that the public interest in free expression and parody outweighed that slight risk of confusion.

In contrast with the *Cliffs Notes* decision, the Eighth Circuit held that a parody involving a mock advertisement on the back of a humor magazine did create confusion. In *Anheuser-Busch, Inc. v. Balducci Publications*,[21] the defendants claimed that the parody was intended to comment on three things: 1) the effects of an oil spill in a river that is the main water source for Anheuser-Busch; 2) Anheuser-Busch's decision to temporarily close its St. Louis facility as a result of that oil spill; and 3) the proliferation of Anheuser-Busch's brands and advertisements. Conversely, the plaintiff argued that the defendant's mock advertisement created a significant likelihood of confusion, and therefore, violated the Lanham Act. In support of this proposition, the plaintiff offered survey evidence to show that over half of those questioned thought that permission would be required to produce such advertisements and that six percent surveyed thought it was an actual Anheuser-Busch advertisement. Despite this evidence, the district court found that the parody was permissible.[22] Specifically, the court gave "special sensitivity" to the First Amendment aspects of the case, while engaging in the confusion analysis. Accordingly, the district court employed a heightened test for confusion and ruled that the editorial nature of the defendant's parody required a greater showing of confusion on the part of the plaintiff.

On appeal, the Eighth Circuit Court of Appeals reversed and held that the district court erred in applying a heightened likelihood of confusion test. The correct standard, is to analyze the likelihood of confusion issue first and then consider the scope of the First Amendment issues. Applying this standard, the

Court of Appeals found that the defendant's mock advertisement created a significant likelihood of confusion. In particular, the court noted that the advertisement appeared on the back of the magazine when the plaintiff's advertisement often appeared in other magazines and the advertisement used identical versions of the Anheuser-Busch marks. Furthermore, the plaintiff's survey evidence was particularly persuasive and strongly indicated actual consumer confusion.

In considering the implications, the *Anheuser-Busch* court noted, as did the *Cliffs Notes* court, that confusion might be tolerated if necessary to achieve the desired commentary. However, the court found in this case that the confusion was completely unnecessary to achieve the defendant's stated purpose. Unlike the commentary in *Cliffs Notes* which conjured up elements of the original but also sent a clear message that it was not the original, in this case defendant's commentary was an unaltered appropriation of the original. The court stated that the defendant had failed to make it clear that its advertisement was a parody, and therefore, unnecessarily created confusion. The court concluded that the balance between the public interest in avoiding consumer confusion and the public interest in free expression weighed against the defendant's First Amendment considerations.

In another case following the *Cliffs Notes* balancing approach to trademark parodies, the Southern District of New York found no likelihood of confusion between the defendant's movie character and the plaintiff's meat product. In *Hormel Foods Corp. v. Jim Henson Productions, Inc.*,[23] the plaintiff, owner of the trademark "SPAM," a meat product, brought a trademark action against the defendant movie producer, who featured a character named Spa'am in its movie. The plaintiff asserted that the use of the character Spa'am in the defendant's movie created a likelihood of confusion and tended to direct negative associations to the plaintiff's product.

The Southern District Court of New York held that the defendant's use of a character named Spa'am did not create a likelihood of confusion with the plaintiff's meat product SPAM. In reaching this decision, the court recognized the standard set forth in *Cliffs Notes* as the appropriate test for addressing a First Amendment defense in a trademark parody context. Following this standard, the court first applied each of the eight factors articulated in *Polaroid Corp. v. Polaroid Electric Corp.*[24] to determine whether there was a likelihood of confusion. The court noted that the defendant's character and the plaintiff's meat product were easily distinguishable and would not confuse consumers. Consequently, the court concluded that there was no likelihood of confusion, and therefore, did not have the occasion to engage in the subsequent First Amendment balancing analysis.

Two district courts have confronted the First Amendment defense in trademark infringement actions and have employed two different standards in reaching their conclusions. In *No Fear, Inc. v. Imagine Films, Inc.*,[25] the plaintiff, a sportswear manufacturer, brought an infringement action the defendant who was making a movie called "No Fear." The defendant filed a motion for summary judgment asserting a First Amendment defense and contending that the use of the title was artistic expression, relying on *Rogers v. Grimaldi*.[26] In particular, the defendant argued that the stringent balancing test applied in *Rogers* was applicable. The court noted, however, that the *Rogers* test, by its own admission, is limited to cases involving the use of celebrity names in the title of works. Thus, the court chose to follow balancing tests articulated in *Cliffs Notes* and *Twin Peaks Productions v. Publications International, Inc.*[27] The court stated that the first part of the analysis is to determine whether there is a likelihood of confusion under the traditional framework; the second part is to weigh the risk of confusion against the First Amendment concerns. Applying this standard, the court concluded that at the summary judgment phase, the parties failed to produce enough evidence to fully evaluate the likelihood and extent of confusion as to the film's source. Accordingly, the court denied the defendant's motion due to the remain questions of fact.

Another case that addressed the parody issue is *Dr. Seuss Enterprises, L.P. v. Penguin Books USA, Inc.*[28] In *Dr. Seuss,* the plaintiff owned the "Dr. Seuss" trademarks. The defendants wrote a story about the O. J. Simpson trial entitled *The Cat NOT in the Hat,* by Dr. Juice. The plaintiff brought a preliminary injunction action, asserting *inter alia,* that the defendant misappropriated several of the plaintiff's marks and created a likelihood of confusion through its parody. Conversely, the defendants claimed that its use was non-infringing. The district court granted the plaintiff's motion for preliminary injunction because the defendant's use of the plaintiff's trademarks raised substantial questions for litigation and the balance of hardships favored the grant of the injunction. The defendants made an interlocutory appeal.

The Court of Appeals for the Ninth Circuit affirmed the district court's holding. The court analyzed the likelihood of confusion issue under the eight factors from *Sleekcraft*.[29] The court concluded that many of these factors were indeterminate; thus, the plaintiff had raised question for litigation. Furthermore, the court recognized that some other courts have issued injunctions for works that poke fun at a trademark. The court noted that the claim of parody is no defense "'where the purpose of the similarity is to capitalize on a famous mark's popularity for the defendant's own commercial use.'"

In granting the plaintiff's motion for a preliminary injunction, the court held that the defendant's use of the plaintiff's trademarks raised substantial questions for litigation and the balance of hardships favored the grant of the injunction. The court first determined that the plaintiff had shown a possibility of confusion, but failed to establish a reasonable likelihood of success on the merits. In reaching this result, the court analyzed the confusion issue under the traditional framework. The court found that although the plaintiff's marks were strong, the plaintiff was unable to establish that the defendant's use was sufficiently similar and that the use would likely lead to confusion among consumers. Specifically, the court took into account the significant steps that the defendant took in order to reduce the likelihood of confusion, such as the label "A Parody" prominently featured on the defendant's packaging and the disclaimer. Thus, the court concluded that although the plaintiff has raised questions for litigation, the plaintiff had not established that the defendant's use had created a likelihood of confusion.

Secondly, the court considered the merits of a possible First Amendment defense. In addressing this issue, the court declined to follow the balancing approach used in *Cliffs Notes* and *Anheuser-Busch*. Rather, the court analyzed this issue under the traditional approach articulated by the *Dallas Cowboys* court. In applying this standard, the court rejected the defendant's First Amendment defense and concluded:

> Just as in copyright, trademark infringement will be excused only where necessary to the purpose of the use. Where alternative avenues of achieving the satiric or parodic ends exist that would not entail consumer confusion, the First Amendment will not protect the parodist from being held to infringe. The court's reasoning as to the fair use defense therefore applies equally to this issue. Dr. Suess would most likely prevail at trial against a First Amendment defense.

Challenges remain and questions linger as to the proper analytical framework in trademark parody cases, as can be seen by the emergence and proliferation in the late 1980s of First Amendment concerns. The First Amendment analysis for trademark parody seems to be evolving into a two-part test. The first part is to determine if the use of the trademark is unlawful, confusing, misleading, or disparaging using the traditional tests for trademark infringement, dilution, or right of publicity. The second part is to determine whether the speech is commercial or non-commercial. If the speech is commercial, no balancing test is required under the First Amendment. Those interests are analyzed in the traditional infringement context. If the speech is non-commercial, the balancing test is required under the First Amendment interests should be balanced. In the context of non-commercial speech, courts will tolerate a higher level of confusion than would otherwise be the case.

Another issue to consider is whether the balancing would be the same in trademark infringement versus dilution or right of publicity. Some commentators have suggested that the trademark owner's interest in avoiding dilution should be given much less weight than the trademark owner's interest in preventing confusion because confusion also involves the public's interest in not being mislead. The *L. L. Bean* case suggests in the context of artistic speech, non-commercial speech that the private interest in preventing dilution should not be weighed against the First Amendment interest.

This Article has identified a framework of analysis that seeks to account for the legitimate yet sometime competing interests of artistic expression and trademark protection. The remaining challenge is to test that framework against future cases. The results in trademark parody cases are sometimes difficult to reconcile. The humor is often simply in the eye of the beholder.

The line between permissible artistic expression and impermissible disparagement and confusion can be difficult for courts to draw. In practice, it seems a plaintiff is most likely to succeed against a trademark parody when the parody is disparaging or offensive, the parody is identical or closely similar to the original trademark, and the interest of the public in avoiding confusion is strong.

PART III
INTERNET

22

DOMAIN NAME DISPUTE RESOLUTION: DEVELOPMENT AND PHILOSOPHY

Domain name disputes began to reach the courts in 1994. As the importance of the Internet as a commercial medium grew, the number of trademark disputes involving domain names grew accordingly. Unfortunately, the existing rules proved inadequate. This paper covers the background and philosophy leading to two developments to address the problem. The ICANN Uniform Dispute Resolution Policy (ICANN UDRP) seeks to resolve such disputes in a quick, cost-effective manner. The Anti-Cybersquatting Consumer Protection Act (ACPA) provides relief under federal law against bad faith registration of domain names.

THE DOMAIN NAME SYSTEM

There are two basic types of top level domains: generic and country code. Generic top level domains, or gTLDs, include .com (commercial), .edu (education), .org (organization), .net (network), .gov (government), .int (international), and .mil (military).

In addition to the generic TLD=s the domain name system hierarchy design included 249 country code TLDs (ccTLDs). The ccTLDs, include such top level domains as .uk (United Kingdom), .it (Italy) and .fr (France). It was the original intent of the system that ccTLDs would be used for local entities. While that has been the case in the majority of ccTLDs, there is a growing trend to operate ccTLDs as open systems which will accept registration from users in any location.

Over 200 ccTLDs accept registrations. In most cases, registration requires a local presence in the particular country. Over 80 ccTLDs, however, accept registrations without regard to location, and thus function in a manner similar to gTLDs. Some of these ccTLDs now promote themselves as alternatives to the ".com" gTLD. For example, the Cocos Islands operates its national domain ".cc" as a gTLD.

DOMAIN NAME DISPUTES

As the commercial importance of the Internet increased, domain names and trademarks have come into conflict, a situation exacerbated by the fact that each domain name must be unique. Unlike the physical world, where identical trademarks can co-exist for different classes of products (*e.g.*, UNITED for airlines, moving vans, and a soccer team), on the Internet there can only be one <united.com>. Some people believe the conflict between trademarks and domain names is also increased by the practice of registering domain names on a first come, first served basis, without an examination process or review.

The nature of the system leads to conflicts between legitimate users of the same name. For example, who should be entitled to the domain name <ritz.com>: Ritz Hotels, Nabisco RITZ crackers or RITZ cameras? The domain name nissan.com was originally held by Uzi Nissan, the operator of a computer business. Mr. Nissan had a legitimate reason for selecting the name, but his use nevertheless prevented the car manufacturer from using its famous mark as its own domain name.

The system also encourages persons without a legitimate interest in a domain name to register the names and marks of others for profit, either by selling the domain name to someone with a legitimate interest or by using the name to direct traffic to a site and increase advertising revenue.

There have been a wide variety of disputes involving domain names. Some of the disputes mirror problems encountered in the physical world. Others are situations unique to the Internet. The various types of disputes include:

Tarnishment. These cases involve the use of a trademark as the domain name for a site with content that damages the reputation of the trademark owner.[1]

Infringement. Traditional disputes between a trademark and a domain name where there is a likelihood of confusion.[2]

Cyberjesters. Early disputes involving the registration of another's name or mark as a domain name.[3]

Cybersquatters. Persons who seek to profit from the registration of the names and marks of others.[4]

Originally, Network Solutions, Inc. ("NSI") was the sole registrar for the .com, .org, and .net gTLDs. The types of problems involving domain names have led to law suits against the registrants and also against NSI. Trademark owners have challenged NSI's granting of a domain name as contributory infringement. NSI has also received law suits from domain name holders faced with challenges from trademark owners.

NSI reacted to the growing number of disputes by adopting a dispute resolution policy that is easy to administer, but does not fully protect the legitimate interests of either domain name holders or trademark owners.

The NSI Policy, which went through several revisions, permitted the owner of a trademark registration to challenge an identical domain name. If the domain name holder could not show a prior registration, NSI would place the domain name on hold until the matter was resolved by settlement or court order.

Some members of the trademark and Internet communities believed the NSI policy was fatally flawed.[5] Trademark owners objected to the NSI policy because (a) NSI did not recognize claims based on common law rights; (b) NSI did not recognize claims based on similar but not identical rights; and (c) because expensive litigation might be required to obtain a transfer of the domain name if the registrant did not cooperate.

Domain name holders objected to the NSI policy because NSI honored claims based on a trademark registration without regard to the nature of the goods or services involved, permitting overreaching by trademark owners.

The NSI policy led to general dissatisfaction and a new class of disputes, known as "reverse domain name hijacking" in which domain name holders objected to the use of the NSI policy by a trademark owner to challenge the use of a domain name for unrelated goods or services.[6]

The perceived problems with the NSI dispute policy led to various reform efforts involving proposed technical and legal solutions.

INTERNATIONAL PROPOSALS FOR DOMAIN NAME SYSTEM REFORM

IAHC Proposals

The International Ad Hoc Committee (IHAC) was founded in 1996 to address concerns arising from the NSI policies.

The IAHC proposals included the introduction of new gTLDs and the creation of a dispute resolution procedure involving the use of Administrative Challenge Panels. The IAHC proposals did not effect the administration of the .com domain. The IAHC was dissolved on May 1, 1997, and the progress of its proposals was arrested by policy statements of the Clinton Administration calling for a new corporation to administer the existing gTLDs and for more study on dispute resolution.[7]

THE CLINTON ADMINISTRATION PROPOSALS

On July 7, 1997, the Department of Commerce published a request for public comment seeking views of the public on the registration and administration of the domain names. On February 20, 1998, the National Telecommunications and Information Administration (NTIA) of the Department of Commerce published a proposed rule regarding the domain name registration system. Known as the "Green Paper," the statement sought comment on the privatization of the domain name system.

On June 5, 1998, the Commerce Department issued the Management of Internet Names and Addresses (or "White Paper"), a Statement of Policy on the privatization of Internet Domain Name System.

The White Paper called for the formation of a new corporation to administer the gTLD domains and asked WIPO to convene an international process and submit recommendations to the new corporation.

ICANN

In October, 1998, The Internet Corporation for the Assigned Names and Numbers (ICANN) submitted a proposal to NTIA to administer the gTLD domains. ICANN was established by the Internet Assigned Names Association (IANA) through a process seeking to develop a consensus within the Internet community for private administration of the domain name system. Although other organizations also submitted proposals, the ICANN proposal gained the broadest support. More information on ICANN is available at http://www.icann.org.

THE WIPO PROCESS

As a result of the request set forth in the White Paper, the World Intellectual Property Organization (WIPO) convened an international process to gather worldwide views on domain name disputes and has assembled a diverse Panel of Experts to advise WIPO during the process.

The final report on the WIPO Internet Domain Name Process entitled "Management of Internet Names and Addresses: Intellectual Property Issues" was published on April 30, 1999. The efforts of WIPO focused on four main areas: dispute prevention; dispute resolution; protection of famous and well-known marks; and the effect of introducing new gTLDs.

The WIPO recommendations covered five basic points:

1. The rights and obligations between the domain name holder and registration authority should be controlled by a written contract.

2. Domain name holders should be required to provide accurate and reliable contract information so that other parties can contact them in the event of a dispute.

3. The domain name contract should require domain name holders to submit to an administrative dispute resolution process.

4. There should be pre-emptive exclusions for famous and well-known marks.

5. New gTLDs should be introduced cautiously, and only if the new domains are clearly differentiated and subject to meaningful dispute resolution procedures.

WIPO DISPUTE POLICY RECOMMENDATIONS

WIPO recommended that the dispute policy focus on abusive domain name registrations. The definition of abusive registration recommended by WIPO was as follows (Final Report, 171):

The registration of a domain name shall be considered to be abusive when all of the following conditions are met:

1. the domain name is identical or misleadingly similar to a trade or service mark in which the complainant has rights; and

2. the holder of the domain name has no rights or legitimate interests in respect of the domain name; and

3. the domain name has been registered and is used in bad faith.

For the purposes of paragraph (1)(iii), the following, in particular, shall be evidence of the registration and use of a domain name in bad faith:

1. an offer to sell, rent or otherwise transfer the domain of the owner of the trade or service mark, for valuable consideration; or

2. an attempt to attract, for financial gain, Internet users to the domain name holder's web site or other on-line location, by creating confusion with the trade or service mark of the complainant; or

3. the registration of the domain name in order to prevent the owner of the trade or service mark from reflecting the mark in a corresponding domain name, provided that a pattern of such conduct has been established on the part of the domain name holder; or

4. the registration of the domain name in order to disrupt the business of a competitor.

A key feature of the WIPO philosophy was the premise that the Policy did not apply to ordinary infringement disputes:

> The cumulative conditions of the first paragraph of the definition make it clear that the behavior of innocent or good faith domain name registrants is not to be considered abusive. For example, a small business that had registered a domain name could show, through business plans, correspondence, reports, or other forms of evidence, that it had a bona fide intention to use the name in good faith. Domain name registrations that are justified by legitimate free speech rights or by legitimate non-commercial considerations would likewise not be considered to be abusive. And, good faith disputes between competing right holders or other competing legitimate interests over whether two names were misleadingly similar would not fall within the scope of the procedure.

ICANN UDRP

May 27,1999, the ICANN Board adopted a resolution referring the recommendations of chapter 3 of the WIPO final report to the ICANN Domain Name Supporting Organization (DNSO). On August 20, 1999, a group of Registrars submitted a model Policy to ICANN, based largely on the WIPO recommendations. On October 24, 1999, the ICANN Board approved the Policy to become effective starting December 1, 1999. The first proceeding under the ICANN UDRP commenced on December 23, 1999.

During the first year of operation, 2741 proceedings were commenced under the ICANN UDRP; and 1905 decisions were issued (1534 in favor of Complainant). As of August 4, 2003, 7309 proceedings had been resolved by decision (5836 resulting in transfer to the Complainant).

A number of ccTLD registrars have adopted the Policy and the procedures were also adopted for the new gTLDs introduced in 2001: .info and .biz.

By most accounts, the ICANN UDRP has proven to be a cost-effective and efficient method of addressing domain name disputes, producing more equitable results than the prior NSI policy. Nevertheless, the Policy continues to face criticism, in part because the decisions have predominantly favored trademark owners over domain name registrants.[8]

ANTI-CYBERSQUATTING CONSUMER PROTECTION ACT

Concerns about the limitations of the Lanham Act to cybersquatting problems led to the enactment in November, 1999 of the Anticybersquatting Consumer Protection Act.[9] The ACPA created a cause of action against anyone who, with bad faith intent to profit from the mark, registers, traffics in, or uses a domain name that is identical or confusingly similar to a distinctive trademark, or is identical or confusingly similar to or dilutive of a famous mark.

The statute contains a non-exhaustive list of factors that a court may consider in determining whether there is bad faith, including:

1. any trademark or other intellectual property rights the alleged violator has in the domain name;

2. whether the domain name is a legal name of the alleged violator or a name commonly used to identify them;

3. the alleged violator's prior use of the domain name in connection with a bona fide offering of goods or services;

4. the alleged violator's intent to create likely confusion and divert customers from the mark owner either for commercial gain or to tarnish or disparage the mark;

5. any offer by the alleged violator to sell or transfer the domain name rights either to the trademark owner or a third party;

6. the alleged violator's use of false or misleading contact information when applying for registration;

7. the alleged violator's registration or acquisition of multiple domain names that the registrant knows are identical or confusingly similar to the distinctive marks of others or dilutive of others' famous marks; and

8. the alleged violator's legitimate non-commercial or fair use of the domain name in a site accessible under the domain name.

The statute allows a court to order the forfeiture or cancellation of the domain name or the transfer of the name to the trademark owner. In addition to the traditional monetary remedies available under the Lanham Act, this amendment also provides for elective statutory damages ranging from $1000 to $100,000 per domain name. The Act applies even to domain names registered before its passage, but the complainant cannot recover damages for pre-Act activities.

CONCLUSION

The Internet poses great challenges and opportunities. It is a considerable challenge to adapt our existing, territorial laws of intellectual property to a global communication and commercial medium that has no boundaries. We need to find a balance between the protection of intellectual property rights, which is necessary if the Internet will reach its full potential as a virtual marketplace, and universal access, which is necessary if the Internet is to reach its full potential as a communications medium. That challenge creates the opportunity to develop international systems for resolving disputes in a way that encourages growth of the Internet. The challenge can best be met through the thoughtful application of traditional trademark principles developed by the courts through the years as they seek to accommodate the competing interests of property protection, competition and free speech. The ICANN UDRP is a positive, cost-effective mechanism for revolving domain name disputes.

PART IV
STRATEGY AND TACTICS

23

TO SUE OR NOT TO SUE

Your client has contacted you about a perceived infringement and wants your advice: to sue or not to sue? The question raises a variety of matters that need to be considered before you take action. This paper will address some of the considerations involved.

PRELIMINARY CONSIDERATIONS

The first step in addressing an infringement problem is to identify the client's goals. Does the client seek money or will it be satisfied with an injunction to halt infringement? Is the client concerned about an encroachment on its rights or does it seek to stop or inhibit competition? Is the client responding to a particular wrong or does it recognize the importance of a general goal of deterring others from infringing conduct?

It is important the you help your client shape realistic goals, otherwise your efforts are destined to fail. To shape and evaluate those goals, you should weigh the risks of litigation against the risks of no action.

One of the risks of litigation is the potential for substituting a financial problem for a legal one. Litigation is expensive and unpredictable. Cost estimates are possible, but the process is akin to trying to build a house while someone else is trying to tear it down. You and your client need to consider whether the legal problem justifies the cost. Can you afford to win? A second risk of litigation is the potential effect of a loss. If you pursue a weak case, will a loss damage your rights against others? Is your trademark at risk of being held generic? Would it be better to begin with stronger cases or weaker opponents?

There are also risks associated with taking no action. Trademark rights can be lost or weakened through acquiescence, thus the failure to take action against one infringer may reduce your ability to prevent more damaging infringements in the future. Also, your client's failure to take action may create a reputation in its industry making it a target for other encroachments.

We encourage our clients to take a strategic approach to the protection of their trademark rights. Rather than merely react to particular infringements when they rise to a level sufficient to inflict competitive damage, it is desirable to investigate and identify potential problems at an early stage and formulate a plan for challenging the infringements before they become major problems. One approach is to take on the easy cases first, building a record of successful consent judgments. Another approach is to pursue a prominent test case where a solid victory will create precedent to deter other infringers. Either way, the favored approach is to develop a consistent, proactive plan rather than a reactive response that varies from case to case.

INVESTIGATION

Before determining a course of action it is important for the attorney to fully investigate the situation. A full understanding of the problem will help you determine what course of action to take. Moreover, the obligations imposed by Rule 11 of the Federal Rules of Civil Procedure require that the attorneys have a good faith basis for the allegations presented in a complaint. Court have imposed sanctions where attorneys have relied solely on the representations of their clients and failed to make an independent investigation of the facts.

Your investigation should be guided by consideration of the matters typically at issue in trademark litigation. Your early investigations should lead to preliminary, good faith conclusions on the following issues that support your decision to file suit. Other matters may also need to be considered.

Protectability. The existence of protectable rights is an essential element of any trademark infringement action. Is the term or device at issue capable of being protected? This may not be immediately apparent if your are dealing with terms in an unfamiliar industry or with product configuration. Your investigations will need to address whether the term is generic, descriptive or arbitrary in the particular industry or whether the device is functional and incapable of protection. If the term or device is capable of protection, is it inherently distinctive? If the device is not inherently distinctive, has there been sufficient use to create secondary meaning?

Priority. It is obviously essential to be sure that your rights are prior to the alleged defendants. First adoption is not necessarily sufficient. Priority can be established through application date, use analogous to trademark use, or technical trademark use in commerce.

Strength of mark. Once prior rights are found, we turn to the key issue of likelihood of confusion, which involves a balance of various factors. Strength refers to the source indicating power of a mark shown through distinctiveness, use, advertising and public aware.

Similarity of marks. In an infringement action, you must consider the marks as they appear to the public. Thus, the context of use on packaging or advertising is important.

Channels of trade. Are the products sold through the same outlets? Is one an institutional product only while the other is sold only to retailers? Likelihood of confusion is increased if the products are sold through the same channels of trade. Confusion may be avoided if the channels are unrelated.

Nature of purchase. This factor involves consideration of the cost of the goods involved, the method of purchase and the characteristics of the purchaser. Confusion is more likely for inexpensive items, purchased on impulse by ordinary consumers than for expensive items purchased after careful deliberation by professional purchasers.

Actual confusion. Although hard to obtain, evidence of actual confusion is the best evidence of a likelihood of confusion. Such evidence can include misdirect mail, returned product, incorrect attribution in the media, comments for competitors or customers. If your client is experiencing actual confusion, you will want to take early steps to document and preserve the evidence.

Intent. While bad intent is in the mind of the defendant, your client may possess circumstantial evidence that supports a finding of intent to trade on its goodwill. Has there been past contact between the parties? Are they direct competitors in a narrow field?

Licensing. After considering the information that supports a finding of prior rights and the likelihood of confusion, you should also consider potential defenses that may be raised against your claims. If the client is involved in licensing, does it exercise quality control? If not, it marks may be at jeopardy for naked licensing, i.e., licensing without quality control, which can result in an abandonment of rights. The naked licensing defense is rarely successful, but it can significantly cloud the issues, reducing your chances for quick relief or a favorable settlement. By investigating the potential problem early, the client may be in a position to mend its ways before the matter becomes a problem.

Ownership. In these times of frequent corporate acquisitions, reorganizations and transfers to holding companies, you should determine that your client is the correct owner of the rights at issues. Mistakes over title are not likely to determine the final merits of the case, but disputes over title can again reduce your chances of quick relief or a favorable settlement.

Genericide. Before bringing suit, you should question your client on whether their mark is at risk of being deemed a generic term. This is particularly important in specialized fields, such as medical or computer technology. The client may have marketing studies that bear on this issue. Misuse of the mark in advertising and promotional materials may also be a problem. The client may want to change its marketing strategies before bring suit.

Laches and acquiescence. How long has your client known of the potential infringement? Undue delay in bringing action may prevent you from obtaining a preliminary injunction or damages.

SOURCES OF INFORMATION

There are a variety of sources of information for your prelitigation investigations.

Witnesses. It is useful to begin your case analysis with interviews of the persons immediately concerned about the problem. What do they see as the problem? Why do they want you too take action? How would they explain the matter to the judge of jury? In the typical consumer products company, the brand manager is likely to be the person immediately concerned about the problem and will be source of evidence throughout the case. In a smaller company, perhaps the president will be the one most concerned about the problem. In any event, your task will be easier if you have the support of the persons most concerned with the problem and can shape your claims and further investigations around the issues that matter to the persons who will be your key witnesses. Cases often flounder when attorneys pursue a case theory that is not fully supported by the persons directly involved with the products at issue.

Client's records. An initial review of the relevant documents held by your client is important. Smoking guns often cool and become insignificant if uncovered early in the investigations. At a minimum, you can avoid shaping a case that is contradicted by your own documents and can develop a favorable spin for those documents that seem damaging. The failure to uncover problem documents early is akin to climbing out on the limb of a large tree, then handing your opponent a saw. In addition to marketing documents relating to the products at issue, you should consider the following categories of documents:

Trademark registration files. Look particularly for positions taken by the client during prosecution that may limit its rights in the mark.

Licensing. Proper licensing may strengthen you client's rights, but improper licensing may weaken the strength of the mark or result in an abandonment of rights.

Market research. Look for brand awareness studies that confirm the strength of the mark at issue; advertising and focus group studies that may provide evidence of actual confusion; brand studies that may bear on genericness.

Sales. In addition to sales data, field sales reports may include instances of actual confusion or reports of product disparagement by your opponent.

Litigation. Look for past decisions affecting the brand, contrary positions taken in other litigation, settlement agreements that limit the scope of your clients rights, prior adverse testimony.

Public records. A great deal of information about the defendant and the strength of your client's rights can be learned through public information sources. Some examples include:

Trademark search. Commercial search reports will include registration, application and common law use information that can help you evaluate priority, the extent of third-party use and the scope of your client's rights.

Dun & Bradstreet reports. Public reports used for credit checks will help you correctly identify the defendant and evaluate the potential for damages. Such reports may also provide information and admissions on the nature of the defendant's business and its first use of the name at issue.

Online information. Nexis searches can be used to obtain information about the defendant's business and first use of the offending mark, as well as information on the fame of your client's mark and the extent of third-party use. The defendant's web site may provide information to evaluate the similarity of the products and channels of trade and the identity of officers and other relevant witnesses.

Government filings. Official records will help you correctly identify the defendant in your pleadings and may also provide admissions by the defendant that help you prove some of the elements of your claims. Some of the place you may want to check are: The Patent and Trademark Office; Secretary of State; SEC; FDA; BATF and others.

Investigators. We often use paralegals or outside investigators to obtain information about the potential defendants, particularly in counterfeiting or gray market goods cases where information about the defendant is not available through public sources. Investigators often obtain information by posing as a potential customer. As long as the investigators do not engage in entrapment, i.e., cause the defendant to commit an infringement it would not otherwise commit, the use of a subterfuge to obtain information should not harm your case or the evidence obtained.

Surveys. The use of survey evidence has become common at trial in trademark infringement cases. Surveys can also be used as an initial case evaluation or settlement tool. We have used attorney-designed and supervised surveys both to evaluate the merits of a potential case and in negotiations with our opponent to induce settlement. Although we would need to have a survey conducted by an independent expert for use at trial, the attorney designed survey is substantially cheaper and can be a very effective too to show your opponent the kind of evidence that you would be able to present if the case goes to trial. The cost of a survey designed and conducted under the supervision of an expert for trial typically costs $30,000 to 50,000, or more, depending on the difficulty of the methodology. In contrast, we find that we can conduct our own mall-intercept study using accepted methodologies for $10,000 to 15,000 or less.

IDENTIFICATION OF THE CLAIMS

Having gathered the necessary information for a full understanding of the problem, we turn next to the identification of the legal claims that may be pursued. In addition to traditional trademark infringement, the problem may give rise to other claims based on the principals of trademark law, including: trade dress; product configuration; counterfeiting; grey market; false advertising, and dilution. There may be state law claims for unfair competition based on the same acts that give rise to federal claims under the Lanham Act. Where logos or trade dress are involved, there may also be claims for copyright infringement. The use of personal identity may raise right of publicity claims. The choice of claims can affect the available remedies and the defenses at issue.

INITIATING THE OBJECTION

The decision to contact your opponent before filing suit arises in every case. The decision is a strategic one: which course will lead most directly to the desired result at the cheapest cost? There is no legal obligation to contact your opponent before filing suit. Moreover, your opponent's complaint to the court that the case was brought without warning will probably fall on deaf ears. The judges know there are many good and sufficient reasons why a party will sue without giving warning. Thus, the failure to give prior warning is not likely to have any adverse affects on the merits of your claims.

In some circumstances, an initial contact by phone or written demand may be the best course to resolve a case quickly. Can your client build on an existing relationship to resolve the matter short of litigation? Sometimes it is easier to resolve before the litigators get involved. Once the complaint is filed, compromise may become more difficult as your opponent consults outside counsel and positions harden. The value of in-house settlement negotiations must be balanced against the risk of litigating in a distant jurisdiction. Threatening litigation may permit your opponent to bring a declaratory judgment action in its home forum. A compromise is to file a complaint at the same time you make your demand, but refrain from service if your opponent agrees to negotiate a prompt settlement.

SELECTING THE FORUM

When deciding to pursue an objection, there are a number of private and public options.

Private resolution of the dispute may be pursued through private negotiations, mediation, arbitration or other forms of ADR which are increasingly used as a means of reducing the time and expense of litigation.

Before selecting federal court litigation, you may also want to consider if your client's goals can be better realized in other types of proceedings. Disputes over pending or registered trademarks can be addressed using opposition or cancellation proceedings before the Trademark Trial and Appeal Board. Such proceedings are generally less expensive than civil litigation and often lead to settlement.

The International Trade Commission offers expedited procedures to deal with unfair competition in the importation of goods. The proceeding operate on a fast track and an investigative attorney participates in discovery and the hearings as an independent party. In the right case, the involvement of the investigative attorney may be a benefit.

Some litigators favor state court actions, believing that threat of litigating in an unfamiliar state court is more intimidating to an opponent that litigating in federal court. Some litigators also believe that some state court judges may have more time and interest in a trademark dispute than their federal court counterparts.

False advertising disputes are often presented to the National Advertising Division of the Better Business Bureau for decision.

Finally, with the growing use of the internet, there is increasing use of the dispute resolution procedures provided by the ICANN UDRP.

AVAILABLE RELIEF

Your selection of forum will partly be controlled by the desired relief. In federal court, the relief available includes: an injunction, actual damages, profits, attorney's fees, product recall, the use of a disclaimer and destruction of infringing materials. A wider range of options is available through settlement or mediation. A private resolution can make creative use of licensing, assignment of rights, label modifications, phase out periods and other business arrangements. In the TTAB, relief is limited to refusal or cancellation of registration. No monetary relief is available.

CONSIDERATIONS FOR LITIGATION

Once you decide to proceed with litigation, there are a number of additional questions to address.

1. Who do we sue? In addition to the corporate defendant, are there individual officers to include in the complaint? When dealing with a small counterfeiter, we try to include individuals in the complaint. Otherwise the value of any injunction may evaporate as the principals form new operations to continue their illegal activities. You may also want to consider the benefit of including suppliers, retailers or distributors as defendants. When dealing with private label problems, for example, clients are often reluctant to sue their own customers. We find such problems can be handled effectively by suing the supplier.

2. Where should we sue? This question goes beyond the formal requirements of personal jurisdiction and venue. There is a wide divergence between the federal courts in terms of local practice. Virginia has the "rocket docket." Illinois has a special mediation program for Lanham Act cases. Some districts have a docket backlog that may delay summary judgment decisions and trial. The Northern District of California has an early neutral evaluation procedure to help resolve disputes. In choosing between courts, you will want to supplement your own research with the advice of a knowledgeable local counsel. We find that the most helpful local counsel is not necessarily an intellectual property lawyer, but rather someone familiar with the courts.

3. What procedures should we pursue? The client's goals may demand that we seek immediate relief. Will that be an ex parte TRO, a TRO with notice or a motion for preliminary injunction? A TRO is most likely to be granted in counterfeiting situations. Either a TRO or preliminary injunction with be a problem if the plaintiff has known of the infringing conduct for a substantial period of time.

4. Should we ask for a jury? Aside from the usual David and Goliath considerations, a jury demand may affect pretrial aspects of a case. A judge may be more reluctant to grant summary judgment if there is a jury demand, but more willing to become involved in settlement efforts.

5. What about insurance? As a plaintiff, there is nothing you can do about insurance coverage, right? Wrong. The possibility of insurance coverage may improve you ability to recover monetary relief. Conversely, it may also result in a vigorous, insurance-funded defense. You can draft your complaint in a way that increases or decreases the likelihood that there will be coverage under the advertising injury clause of a typical general comprehensive liability policy.

CONCLUSION

The decision to sue involves many objective and subjective considerations. Your role as counsel is to see that these matters are fully considered before taking action. We find that happy clients and successful litigation result from thorough communication and preparation before the complaint is filed.

ABOUT THE AUTHOR

Mark Partridge, a graduate of Harvard Law School, has specialized in intellectual property law since 1981. He is a partner in the Chicago office of Pattishall, McAuliffe, Newbury, Hilliard & Geraldson, and an adjunct professor at The John Marshall Law School, where he teaches advanced courses in trademark law, trademark transactions and trademark litigation.

He has served on the Board of Directors for the American Intellectual Property Law Association, is a past president of the Lawyers Club of Chicago, and was selected by the World Intellectual Property Organization to serve on its Panel of Experts for the Internet Domain Name Process.

He lives in the Lincoln Park neighborhood of Chicago.

NOTES

Understanding Substantial Similarity and Scope of Protection

1. See *Feist Publication, Inc., v. Rural Telephone Service Co.,* 499 U.S. 340 (1991).

2. *See, e.g., Repp v. Webber,* 132 F.3d 882, 889 (2d Cir. 1997)(noting the considerable confusion caused by the use of the term "substantial similarity" for two different tests).

3. 17 U.S.C. 102(b).

4. *Kregos v. Associated Press,* 937 F.2d 700, 710 (2d Cir. 1991). *See also Harbor Software, Inc. v. Applied Systems, Inc.,* 936 F. Supp. 167, 171 (S.D.N.Y. 1996)(applying the "trivial difference" test to computer screen displays which were compilations of factual information).

5. See, for example, *Mitek Holdings Inc. v. Arce Engineering Co.,* 89 F.3rd 1548, 1554 (11th Cir. 1996); *Apple Computer Inc. v. Microsoft Corporation,* 35 F.3d 1435, 1446 (9th Cir.1994).

Insufficient Evidence of Originality

1. 133 F.3d 773 (10th Cir. 1998).

2. 499 U.S. 340 (1991).

Damages for Extraterritorial Copyright Infringement

1. 149 F.3d 987 (9th Cir. 1998).

2. 106 F.2d 45 (2d Cir. 1939).

3. See *Subafilms, Ltd. v. MGM-Pathe Communications Co.*, 24 F.3d 1088 (9th Cir. 1994).

4. 47 U.S.P.Q.2d 1764 (S.D.N.Y. 1998).

Choice of Law In International Copyright Disputes

1. 153 F.3d 82 (2d Cir. 1998).

2. 17 U.S.C. §104(c).

The Dimensions of the Fair Use Defense

1. 17 U.S.C. §107.

2. *Id.*

3. 142 F.3d 194 (4th Cir. 1998).

4. 5 F. Supp. 2d 823 (C.D. Cal. 1998).

5. 137 F.3d 109 (2d Cir. 1998).

6. 510 U.S. 569 (1994) .

Comparative Advertising and the Fair Use Defense

1. 214 F.3d 1022 (9th Cir. 2000).

2. 17 U.S.C. §107.

3. 510 U.S. 569 (1994).

Determining Copyright Damages

1. *Mason v. Montgomery Data, Inc.*, 967 F.2d 135 (5th Cir. 1992).

2. 670 F. Supp. 1133, 1139 (E.D.N.Y. 1987).

3. 313 F. Supp. 990, 996 (E.D.N.Y. 1970).

4. 13 F.3d 559 (2d Cir. 1994).

5. 13 F.3d at 564–66.

6. 13 F.3d at 566.

7. 309 U.S. 390 (1940).

8. 712 F.2d 1112, 1120 (7th Cir. 1983).

Copyright Preemption on the Internet

1. See, for example, "Factual Databases: Applying Traditional Legal Theories to Contemporary Internet-Related Issues," *IP Litigator* (July/August 2000).

2. 54 U.S.P.Q.2d 1344 (C.D. Cal. 2000).

3. 100 F.Supp.2d 1058 (N.D. Cal. 2000).

4. 17 U.S.C. §301.

5. Following *Thrifty-Tel v. Bezenek*, 46 Cal. App. 4th 1559 (4th Dist. 1996).

6. See *Thrifty-Tel v. Bezenek*, 46 Cal. App. 4th 1559, 1566 (4th Dist. 1996).

Derivative Works in the Digital Age

1. 207 F.3d 1119 (9th Cir. 2000).

Infringement as the Key to Rights In Derivative Works

1. 207 F.3d 402 (7th Cir. 2000).

2. 17 U.S.C. §101.

3. 17 U.S.C. §103(b).

4. 17 U.S.C. §106(2).

5. 697 F.2d 27 (2d Cir. 1982).

The Limitation Period for Copyright Claims

1. 230 F.3d 518 (2d Cir. 2000).

2. 17 U.S.C. §507(b).

3. 380 U.S. 434 (1965).

4. *International Union of Elec., Radio and Mach. Workers v. Robbins & Myers, Inc.*, 428 U.S. 229 (1976).

5. *Kregos v. The Associated Press*, 3 F.3d 656 (2d Cir. 1993).

6. *Taylor v. Meirick*, 712 F.2d 1112 (7th Cir. 1983); *Woods Hole Oceanographic Institute v. Goldman*, 228 U.S.P.Q. 874 (S.D.N.Y. 1985).

7. *Stone v. Williams*, 970 F.2d 1043 (2d Cir. 1992).

The First Sale Doctrine

1. 523 U.S. 135 (1978).

2. 15 U.S.C. §602.

3. 15 U.S.C. §109(a).

4. An early example of the problem decided by the Supreme Court is *A. Bourjois & C. v. Katzel*, 260 U.S. 689 (1923).

5. *Monte Carl Shirt, Inc. v. Daemo Int'l (America) Corp.*, 707 F.2d 1054 (9th Cir. 1983).

6. *CBS, Inc. v. Scorpion Music Distributors*, 569 F.Supp. 47 (E.D. Pa. 1983), aff'd 738 F.2d 421 (3rd Cir. 1984).

7. *Societe Des Produits Nestle S.A. v. Casa Helvetia, Inc.*, 25 U.S.P.Q.2d 1256 (1st. Cir. 1992).

Threats of Litigation

1. *Computer Aid, Inc. v. Hewlett-Packard*, 56 F.Supp.2d 526 (E.D. Pa. 1999).

2. 182 F.3d 1132 (10th Cir. 1999).

3. *Professional Real Estate Investors, Inc. v. Columbia Pictures, Inc.*, 508 U.S. 49, 60–61 (1993).

4. 634 F. Supp. 316 (D. Kan. 1986).

5. *Thermos Co. v. Igloo Products Corp.*, No. 93 C 5826, 1995 WL 842002, at *3 (N.D. Ill. Sept. 27, 1995) (holding that cease and desist letters were protected activity); *Matsushita Electronics Corp. v. Loral Corp.*, 974 F. Supp. 345, 359 (S.D.N.Y. 1997) (holding that post-litigation letters threatening litigation were privileged and could not be the basis of a tortuous interference claim).

Likelihood of Confusion: Understanding Trademark Law's Key Principle

1. 15 U.S.C. §1141(1).

2. 15 U.S.C. §1125(a)(1)(A).

3. 247 F.407 (1917).

4. *Helene Curtis Industries, Inc. v. Suave Shoe Corp.*, 13 U.S.P.Q.2d 1618 (T.T.A.B. 1989).

5. 520 F.2d 499 (1st Cir. 1975).

6. 15 U.S.C. §1114(1), amended 1962.

7. 799 F.2d 867, 872–873 (2d Cir. 1986).

8. *See e.g. U.S. v. Hon.* 904 F.2d 803 (2d Cir. 1990). *cert. denied*, 498 U.S. 1069 (1991)(jury could consider likelihood of confusion of general public, not just purchasing public): *U.S. v. Yamin*, 868 F.2d 130, 133 (5th Cir.). *cert. denied*, 492 U.S. 924 (1989) (no error where jury was instructed to find

liability if general public, not just potential purchasers, likely to be confused): *U.S. v. Torkington*, 812 F.2d 1347, 1352–1353 (11th Cir. 1987)(likelihood of confusion encompasses post-sale confusion).

9. 523 F.2d 1331, 1341–42 (2d Cir. 1975).

10. 818 F.2d 254, 257–58 (2d Cir 1987).

11. 109 F.3d 1394, 1405 (9th Cir. 1997).

12. 174 F.3d 1036 (9th Cir. 1999).

13. *See Steele v. Bulova Watch Co.*, 344 U.S. 280 (1952).

14. *Nintendo of America, Inc. v. Aeropower Company, Ltd.*, 34 F.3d 246 (4th Cir. 1994).

15. *Reebok International, Ltd. v. Marnatech Enterprises, Inc.*, 970 F.2d 552 (9th Cir. 1992).

16. 344 U.S. 280 (1952).

17. Id.

18. 970 F.2d 552 (9th Cir. 1992).

19. 234 F.2d 633(2nd Cir. 1956).

20. 14 F.3d 824 (2nd Cir. 1994).

21. *Kellogg Co. v. National Biscuit Co.*, 305 U.S. 111 (1938).

22. *Merchant & Evans, Inc. v. Roosevelt Building Products Co.*, 963 F.2d 628, 637–38 (3rd. Cir. 1992); *Country Floors, Inc. v. Gepner*, 930 F.2d 1056 (3rd. Cir. 1991).

23. *A&H Sportswear Inc. v. Victoria Secret Stores, Inc.*, 166 F.3d 197 (3rd Cir. 1999)(en banc)

24. 540 F.2d 266, 279 (7th Cir. 1976).

25. 220 U.S.P.Q. 386 (7th Cir. 1983).

26. 287 F.2d 492, 495 (2d Cir. 1961).

27. *Thompson Medical Company, Inc. v. Pfizer, Inc.*, 753 F.2d 208, 214 (2d Cir. 1985).

28. 867 F.2d 22, 29, (1ˢᵗ Cir. 1989).

29. 930 F.2d 277, 293 (3d Cir. 1991).

30. 870 F.2d 1176, 1185 (7ᵗʰ Cir. 1989).

31. 743 F.2d 1508, 1514 (11ᵗʰ Cir. 1984).

32. 805 F.2d 920, 925 (10ᵗʰ Cir. 1986).

33. 476 F.2d 1357, 1361 (C.C.P.A. 1973).

34. 15 U.S.C. §1125(c).

35. 15 U.S.C. §1125(d).

36. 99 F.3d 244 (7ᵗʰ Cir. 1996).

37. 305 U.S. 111 (1938).

Trade Dress Protection and the Problem of Distinctiveness

1. *See, e.g.*, Blue Bell, Inc. v. Farah Mfg. Co., 508 F.2d 1260, 1265 (5th Cir. 1975) ("The primary, perhaps singular purpose of a trademark is to provide a means for the consumer to separate or distinguish one manufacturer's goods from those of another.").

2. *See, e.g.*, Scarves by Vera, Inc. v. Todo Imps. Ltd., 544 F.2d 1167, 1172 (2d Cir. 1976) ("The trademark laws protect...the senior user's interest...in protecting the good reputation associated with his mark from the possibility of being tarnished by inferior merchandise of the junior user...").

3. *See, e.g.*, Two Pesos, Inc. v. Taco Cabana, Inc., 505 U.S. 763, 773 (1992) ("[T]he protection of trademarks and trade dress under § 43(a) serves the...statutory purpose of preventing...unfair competition.").

4. *E.g.*, *Blue Bell*, 508 F.2d at 1265.

5. *See, e.g.*, Vittoria N. Am., L.L.C. v. Euro-Asia Imps. Inc., 278 F.3d 1076, 1082 (10th Cir. 2001) ("A trademark symbolizes the public's confidence or 'goodwill' in a particular product.") (quoting Premier Dental Prods. Co. v. Darby Dental Supply Co., 794 F.2d 850, 853 (3d Cir. 1986)).

6. 505 U.S. 763 (1992).

7. 529 U.S. 205 (2000).

8. *Two Pesos*, 505 U.S. at 764 n.1.

9. Nabisco, Inc. v. PF Brands, Inc., 50 F. Supp. 2d 188, 199 (S.D.N.Y. 1999).

10. Qualitex Co. v. Jacobson Prods. Co., 514 U.S. 159, 166 (1995) (holding that color per se was protectable).

11. O.&W. Thum Co. v. Dickinson, 245 F. 609, 611 (6th Cir. 1917).

12. Hat Corp. of Am. v. D.L. Davis Corp., 4 F. Supp. 613, 622 (D. Conn. 1933).

13. Fr. Milling Co. v. Washburn-Crosby Co., 7 F.2d 304, 305 (2d Cir. 1925).

14. Mishawaka Rubber & Woolen Mfg. Co. v. S.S. Kresge Co., 316 U.S. 203, 205 (1942).

15. Abercrombie & Fitch Co. v. Hunting World, Inc., 537 F.2d 4, 7 (2d Cir. 1976).

16. 659 F.2d 695 (Former 5th Cir. 1981).

17. *See, e.g.*, AmBrit, Inc. v. Kraft, Inc., 812 F.2d 1531, 1535 n.13, 1535–36 (11th Cir. 1986) (adopting the Fifth Circuit's approach in *Chevron*, stating that "the plaintiff must establish that its trade dress is inherently distinctive or has acquired secondary meaning"); Blau Plumbing, Inc. v. S.O.S. Fix-It, Inc., 781 F.2d 604, 608 (7th Cir. 1986) ("If any of these cases stands for the broader proposition that secondary meaning must be shown even if the trade dress is a distinctive, identifying mark, then we think they are wrong, for the reasons explained by…the Fifth Circuit in *Chevron*."). *But see, e.g.*, Stormy

Clime Ltd. v. ProGroup, Inc., 809 F.2d 971, 974 (2d Cir. 1987) (stating that for § 43(a) protection, a "plaintiff must show that the trade dress of its product has acquired secondary meaning in the marketplace").

18. 505 U.S. 763 (1992).

19. *See, e.g.*, Vibrant Sales, Inc. v. New Body Boutique, Inc., 652 F.2d 299, 304 (2d Cir. 1981) ("Since plaintiff concededly made no attempt to adduce any evidence that its product's appearance…had acquired secondary meaning, its Lanham Act claim should have been dismissed.").

20. 155 F.3d 526 (5th Cir. 1998).

21. *Id.* (citations and internal quotation marks omitted).

22. 51 F.3d 780 (8th Cir. 1995).

23. 568 F.2d 1342 (C.C.P.A. 1977).

24. *See, e.g.*, Ashley Furniture Indus., Inc. v. SanGiacomo N.A. Ltd., 187 F.3d 363, 371 (4th Cir. 1999) ("[D]ifficulties in applying *Abercrombie* to product configuration can often be mitigated by considering the principles stated in *Seabrook*…"); I.P. Lund Trading ApS v. Kohler Co., 163 F.3d 27, 33 (1st Cir. 1998) ("In analyzing inherent distinctiveness in the context of product design, we hold that while the well-known *Abercrombie* test provides a useful analogy, strict application of the test is not required; we reiterate this court's adherence to the *Seabrook Foods* test."); Landscape Forms, Inc. v. Columbia Cascade Co., 113 F.3d 373, 378 n.3 (2d Cir. 1997) ("The questions posed in *Seabrook*…may, in different contexts, be useful tools to assess whether a design is 'likely to be perceived as a source indicator.'"); Wiley v. Am. Greetings Corp., 762 F.2d 139, 141 (1st Cir. 1985) (applying the *Seabrook Foods* factors).

25. The Court of Customs and Patent Appeals is a predecessor court of the Court of Appeals for the Federal Circuit.

26. 40 F.3d 1431, 1434 (3d Cir. 1994).

27. 529 U.S. 205 (2000).

28. *Qualitex Co. v. Jacobson Prods. Co.*, 514 U.S. 159, 164 (1995).

Using Patents and Copyrights To Create Strong Brands

1. 35 U.S.C. §154(a).

2. 35 U.S.C. §171, 173.

3. 17 U.S.C. §304; *Eldred v. Ashcroft*, 123 S.Ct. 769 (2003).

4. 15 U.S.C. §1052(f).

5. *Two Pesos, Inc. v. Taco Cabana, Inc.*, 112 S.Ct. 2753 (1992).

6. *Wal-Mart Stores, Inc. v. Samara Brothers, Inc.*, 120 S.Ct. 1339 (2000).

7. 15 U.S.C. §1125(c).

8. 85 F.2d 75 (2d Cir. 1936).

9. 305 U.S. 111 (1938).

10. 120 S.Ct. 1339 (2000).

11. *Traffix Devices, Inc. v. Marketing Displays, Inc.*, 532 U.S. 23 (2001).

12. 15 U.S.C. §1125(a)(3).

13. *Inwood Laboratories, Inc. v. Ives Laboratories, Inc.*, 102 S.Ct. 2182 (1982).

14. *Qualitex Co. v. Jacobson Products Co.*, 514 U.S. 159 (1995).

15. 870 F.2d 512 (9th Cir. 1989).

16. 58 F.3d 1498 (10th Cir. 1995).

17. See *W.T. Rogers v. Keene*, 778 F.2d 334 (7th Cir. 1985)(stating in dicta the general rule that design patent protection does not prevent the enforcement of a common law trademark in a design feature).

18. See *Kieselstein-Cord v. Accessories by Pearl, Inc.*, 632 F.2d 989 (2d Cir. 1980)(holding that belt buckle design was protectable because it contained an sculptural aspect conceptually separable from the articles function as a

buckle); *Brandir International, Inc. v. Cascade Pacific Lumber Co.*, 834 F.2d 1142 (2d Cir. 1987)(holding that a bike rack design was not protectable because the design was not conceptually separable from the product's function).

19. See Denicola, *Applied Art and Industrial Design: A Suggested Approach to Copyright in Useful Articles*, 67 Minn.L.Rev. 707 (1983).

Trademark Licensing in a Corporate Transaction

1. *Macmahan Pharmacal Co. v. Denver Chem. Mfg. Co.*, 113 F. 468 (8th Cir. 1901).

2. *Dawn Donut Co. v. Hart's Food Stores, Inc.*, 267 F.2d 358 (1959).

3. *Transgo, Inc. v. Ajac Transmission Parts Corp.*, 768 F. 2d 1001 (9th Cir. 1985)(reliance on licensee to maintain quality was adequate control due to ten year association between licensor and licensee).

4. For example of recent cases where the principle resulted in a loss of rights, see *First Interstate Bancorp v. Stenquist*, 16 U.S.P.Q.2d 1704 (N.D. Cal. 1990); *Kortez v. Heffernan*, 1993 U.S. Dist. LEXIS 1846 (N.D. Ill 1993); *Stanfield v. Osborne Industries, Inc.*, 1993 U.S. Dist. LEXIS 18612 (D. Kan. 1993).

5. *Taco Cabana Int'l, Inc. v. Two Pesos, Inc.*, 932 F.2d 1113, 1121 (5th Cir. 1991), aff'd on other grounds, 112 S.Ct. 2753 (1992).

6. See Hawes, *Trademark Licensing Can Lead To Product Liability*, 34 Practical Lawyer 23 (1988); *Crinkley v. Holiday Inns, Inc.*, 844 F.2d 156 (4th Cir. 1988).

7. *Heaton Enterprises of Nevada v. Lang*, 7 U.S.P.Q. 2d 1842 (T.T.A.B. 1988).

8. *Gentry Canning Company v. Blue Ribbon Growers, Inc.*, 138 U.S.P.Q. 536 (T.T.A.B. 1963).

9. *Gould Engineering Co. v. Goebel*, 68 N.E.2d 702 (Mass. S.Ct. 1946).

10. *Texaco, Inc. v. Kane County Oil, Inc.*, 238 N.E.2d 622 (Ill. App. 1968).

11. *California Fruit Growers Exchange v. Sunkist Baking Co.*, 166 F.2d 971 (7th Cir. 1947).

12. *Campbell Soup Co. v. Armour & Co.*, 175 F.2d 795 (3d Cir. 1949).

13. *In re Diamond Walnut Growers Inc.*, 204 U.S.P.Q. 507 (T.T.A.B. 1979).

14. *The Ritz Hotel v. Charles of the Ritz*, 12 IRP 417 (1989)(Australia).

Validity of Registration Not Revived After Abandonment

1. *Nabisco Brands, Inc.* v. *Keebler Company*, Cancellation No. 21,498, June 29, 1995.

2. 15 U.S.C. §1127.

Trademark Parody and the First Amendment: Humor in the Eye of the Beholder

1. See e.g., *Hard Rock Café Licensing Corp. v. Pacific Graphics, Inc.*, 776 F. Supp. 1454, 1462 (W.D. Wash. 1991) (rejecting the defendant's argument that its use of HARD RAIN CAFÉ on T-shirts was a permissible parody of the Hard Rock Café); *Schieffelin & Co. v. Jack Company of Boca, Inc.*, 725 F. Supp. 1314, 1324 (S.D.N Y. 1989)(rejecting defendant's argument that their product was a harmless parody, nothing that the parody was not sufficiently effective to eliminate the likelihood of confusion among the consumers); *Gucci Shops, Inc. v. R. H. Macy & Co.*, 446 F. Supp. 838, 840 (S.D.N.Y. 1977)(enjoining the defendant from marketing diaper bags under the trademark 'Gucchi Goo' because of similarity with the 'Gucci' trademark).

2. See, e.g., *Tin Pan Apple Inc. v. Miller Brewing Co.*, 737 F. Supp. 826, 834 (S.D.N.Y. 1990)(rejecting defendant's parody defense). *Cf. Everready Battery Co. v. Adolph Coors Co.*, 765 F. Supp. 440, 450 (N.D. Ill. 1991)(denying relief to the plaintiff and noting that it was clear that the parody was not the original trademark).

3. *See, e. g., Anheuser-Busch, Inc. v. Balducci Publications,* 28 F.3d 769, 775 (8th Cir. 1994), *cert. denied,* 115 S.Ct. 903 (1995)(expressing concern that the public may be misled by the parody); *Cliffs Notes, Inc. v. Bantam Doubleday Dell Publishing Group, Inc.,* 886 F.2d 490, 495 (2d Cir. 1989)(holding that the public interest in parody outweighed the risk of confusion between Spy Notes and Cliff Notes).

4. *Hormel Foods Corp. v. Jim Henson Prod., Inc.,* No. 95 Civ. 5473, 1995 U.S. Dist. LEXIS 13886, at *21 (S.D.N.Y. Sept. 22, 1995), *aff'd,* 73 F.3d 497 (2d Cir. 1996).

5. U. S. CONST. amend I. "Congress shall make no law...abridging the freedom of speech, or of the press..." *Id.*

6. However, some courts have chosen to ignore the first amendment issue altogether when deciding a trademark parody case. *See, e.g., Jordache Enters. v. Hogg Wyld, Ltd.,* 828 F.2d 1482, 1490 n.7 (1987)(first amendment issue noted in the footnote but not dealt with in the text).

7. The likelihood of confusion test is found in § 32(1) of the Lanham Act 15 U.S.C. § 1114 (1)(1988).

8. *Hormel Foods Corp. v. Jim Henson Prod. Inc.,* No. 95 Civ. 5473, 1995 U.S. Dist. LEXIS 13886, at *13–14 (S.D.N.Y. Sept. 22, 1995), *aff'd.* 73 F.3d 497 (2d Cir. 1996).

9. 407 U.S. 551 (1972). One commentator has argued that *Tanner* should not have been controlling in trademark parody cases because it involved a different form of property, namely real estate. Arlen V. Langvardt, *Protected Marks and Protected Speech: The First Amendment Boundaries in Trademark Parody Cases,* 36 VILL. I. REV. 1, 61 (1991). The issue in *Tanner* was whether a privately owned shopping center could prohibit the distribution of handbills on its property when the handbilling was unrelated to the shopping center's operations. *Tanner,* 407 U.S. at 552. The Court held that the petitioner's privately owned shopping center was not dedicated to public use, and as such, there was no First Amendment right to distribute handbills on the property. *Id.* at 570. The focus of the Court's reasoning centered on the existence of "adequate alternative avenues of communication." *Id.* at 567. Where such 'avenues' existed, property owners did not have to yield to others' exercise of their First Amendment rights. *Id.* at 567.

10. 604 F.2d 200 (2d Cir. 1979). In Dallas Cowboys Cheerleaders, the plaintiffs alleged that when the defendants advertised and exhibited the film "Debbie Does Dallas," they infringed and diluted the plaintiffs' trademark in the Dallas Cowboy cheerleader uniform. *Id.* at 202.

11. *Id.* at 205. Specifically, the court stated that there was a sufficient likelihood that people who would watch the defendant's sexually explicit film would thereafter associate it with the Dallas Cowboy Cheerleaders. *Id.* This association, the court reasoned, would result in confusion that might injure the plaintiff's business reputation. *Id.*

12. 836 F.2d 397 (8th Cir. 1985), *cert. denied*, 488 U.S. 933 (1988).

13. *Rubin v. Coors Brewing Co.*, 115 S.Ct. 1585, 1589 (1995).

14. 425 U.S. 748 (1980).

15. 811 F.2d at 26.

16. 725 F.Supp. 1314 (S.D.N.Y. 1989).

17. The Northern District of Illinois reached a similar decision when the Coca-Cola Company sued a bubble gum company that used a container to market its product which closely resembled a Coca-Cola bottle. *Coca-Cola Co. v. Alma Leo U.S.A., Inc.*, 719 F.Supp. 725 (N.D. Ill. 1989). There, the court examined the distinctive nature of the Coca-Cola container and applied, in reaching its determination, factors such as the commonness of the trademark, the length of time the mark has been used, the scope of advertising and promotion, the nature and extent of the business, and its reputation. *Id.* at 727.

18. 698 F.2d 831 (6th Cir. 1983).

19. The court held that the defendants could not use the "Here's Johnny" phrase based upon a right of publicity theory rather than a traditional likelihood of confusion test. According to the Court, the defendants did not violate the confusion test because it was unlikely that the public would believe that Johnny Carson endorsed or promoted the company's product.

20. *Cliffs Notes, Inc., v. Bantam Doubleday Dell Publishing Group, Inc.*, 886 F.2d 490, 495 (2d Cir. 1989).

21. *Anheuser-Busch, Inc., v. Balducci Publications,* 28 F.3d 769 (8th Cir. 1994), *cert. denied,* 115 S.Ct. 903 (1995).

22. *Anheuser-Busch, Inc. v. Balducci Productions,* 814 F.Supp. 791, 797 (E.D. Mo. 1993), *rev'd.* 28 F.3d 769 (8th Cir. 1994), *cert. denied,* 115 S.Ct. 903 (1995).

23. *Hormel Foods v. Jim Henson Food Prod., Inc.,* No. 95 Civ. 5473, 1995 U. S. Dist. LEXIS 13886, at *23 (S.D.N.Y. Sept. 22, 1995), *aff'd.* 73 F.3d 497 (2d Cir. 1996).

24. 287 F.2d 492 (2d Cir. 1961).

25. 930 F. Supp. 1381 (C.D. Cal. 1995).

26. 875 F.2d 994 (2d Cir. 1989).

27. 996 F.2d 1366 (2d Cir. 1993).

28. 109 F.3d 1394 (S.D. Cal. 1997).

29. Citing *AMF Inc. v. Sleekcraft Boats,* 599 F. 2d 341 (9th Cir. 1979).

Domain Name Dispute Resolution: Development and Philosophy

1. For example, *Hasbro Inc. v. Internet Entertainment Group Ltd.,* 40 U.S.P.Q.2d 1479 (W.D. Wash. 1996)(preliminary injunction granted against use of candyland.com domain name for sexually explicit web site); *Toys 'R' Us Inc. v. Akkaoui,* 40 U.S.P.Q.2d 1836 (N.D. Ca. 1996)(preliminary injunction granted against use of adultsrus.com to sell sexual devices and clothing over the Internet).

2. For example, *Comp Examiner Agency v. Juris Inc.,* 1996 WL 376600 (C.D. Ca. 1996)(preliminary injunction against juris.com domain name for legal software based on prior use of JURIS mark for law office management software).

3. See Joshua Quitner, *Billions Registered: Right Now. There Are No Rules to Keep You From Owning a Bitchin' Corporate Name as Your Own Internet*

Address. Wired, Oct. 1994 (describing journalists acquisition of the domain name <mcdonalds.com>).

4. For example, *Intermatic Inc. v. Toeppen,* 947 F. Supp. 1227 (N. D. Ill. 1996)(Dennis Toeppen registers and offers for sale the domain name intermatic.com); *Panavision Int'l L.P. v. Toeppen,* 945 F. Supp. 1296 (C.D. Ca. 1996)(Toeppen enjoined from use of panavision.com).

5. For a thorough summary of the defects see the NSI Flawed Domain Name Policy Information page at http://www.patents.com/nsi.htm.

6. Examples include: *Interstellar Starship Services, Ltd. v. Epix, Inc.,* 983 F.Supp. 1331 (D.Ore. 1997); *Giacalone v. Network Solutions, Inc.,* (N.D. Ca. 1996).

7. More information about the IAHC and the resulting Generic Top Level Domain Name Memorandum of Understanding, or gTLD-MoU, is available at http://www.iahc.org and at http://www.gtld-mou.org.

8. For a detailed discussion see Helfer and Dinwoodie, "Designing No-National Systems: The Case of the Uniform Domain Name Dispute Resolution Policy," William and Mary Law Review, vol. 43, no. 1 (October 2001).

9. 15 U.S.C. §1125.

0-595-65957-8

Printed in the United States
23233LVS00002B/112

9 780595 659579